OTHER WORKS
BY CLAUDIA ARP

Almost 13
Sanity in the Summertime
Ten Dates for Mates
60 One-Minute Marriage Builders
60 One-Minute Family Builders
60 One-Minute Memory Builders
Mom's Support Group Video Package
Mom's & Dad's Support Group Video Package

Beating THE Winter Blues

The complete survival handbook for moms

Claudia Arp

❖ *A Janet Thoma Book* ❖

THOMAS NELSON PUBLISHERS
Nashville

❖ *A Janet Thoma Book* ❖

Published in Nashville, Tennessee, by Thomas Nelson, Inc., and distributed in Canada by Lawson Falle, Ltd., Cambridge, Ontario.

Scripture quotations are from the NEW KING JAMES VERSION of the Bible. Copyright © 1979, 1980, 1982, Thomas Nelson, Inc., Publishers.

Library of Congress Cataloging-in-Publiction Data

Arp, Claudia.
    Beating the winter blues : a complete survival
handbook for moms / Claudia Arp.
        p.   cm.
    ISBN 0-8407-3318-6
    1. Child rearing—United States.   2. Creative
activities and seat work.   3. Family recreation—
United States.   I. Title.
    HQ769.A775   1991
    649'.1—dc20   91-17234
                                            CIP

Printed in the United States of America
1 2 3 4 5 6 7 — 96 95 94 93 92 91

To all the Moms who have participated in MOM's Support Groups across the United States and in Europe. May this book add more fun to your active parenting years!

Contents

Acknowledgments

Any attempt to list all who gave input would be incomplete. However, I especially want to acknowledge and express appreciation to the following people:

To Sherri Gardner Howell, who helped all along the way with creative, practical insights of life with two children, and for her expertise and editing skills.

To my editor and friend, Janet Thoma, who was always available to answer my questions and to encourage me.

To Steve Bjorkman and Danny Wilson for their artistic contributions to this book.

To our sons and daughters-in-law for allowing me to share family memories.

To Cary Slatery, Susan Farris, Nancy Miller, Jan McKinney, and the many others in MOM's Support Groups who shared their own gems of wisdom and tips for beating the winter blues!

Part One

Getting Started

1

Beating the Winter Blues

"The storm is coming!" Those four words filled me with dread and apprehension. This was our first winter back in Tennessee after living for many years in Austria. We were familiar with Austrian winter storms—but Austria, unlike Tennessee, is prepared for all kinds of winter weather, and life goes on normally.

Not so in East Tennessee! The first winter storm moved closer by the minute. The local weather radio station announced that someone had actually sighted the storm thirty miles west of Knoxville—and it was coming!

The grocery stores, packed with frantic shoppers, resembled after-Christmas clearance sales when shelves are stripped of bargains. The hardware stores sold out of kerosene heaters. We got one too—you can't use electric heaters if the electricity is off. Who knew what might happen—the soothsayers were predicting the worst!

The prospect of no school elated our three boys, and frankly, I imagined scenes of family closeness and togetherness as we

3

snuggled around the cheery fireplace, roasted marshmallows, played Monopoly by candlelight—all happy weather hostages secluded from the busy outside world. The Arps were prepared. Let it snow, let it snow, let it snow! Then we learned about East Tennessee "hype." The storm never arrived!

I remember another prediction that was equally misguided. When my husband, Dave, and I left for the radio studio across town to record programs for "The Family Workshop," the sun was shining. It was a crisp, cold winter day. As we entered the radio station we observed a few stray snowflakes. *No problem,* we thought. On this day there were no forecasts or sightings of winter storms.

Imagine our surprise as we left the studio and discovered that those few flakes had multiplied into many inches of snow, and there was bedlam on the roads! Two hours later we arrived home, totally unnerved, but in one piece.

Anticipation of a winter season always reminds me of both snow-forecasting mishaps. We dread the unknown just as we fear a storm that never arrives. At other times we fail to plan and unforeseen snowstorms catch us unprepared. The storms are coming! You can count on that. Blustery days, snow days, sick days, rainy, muddy, dreary winter blue days. And don't forget holidays. Without preplanning, Christmas can sweep in like a tornado and leave behind family-style debris—empty or overextended bank accounts (Who ever invented lines of credit anyway?); shattered storybook dreams of the perfect Christmas; Dad with four new ties he will never wear; and Mom with five new pounds she can't get off!

Sometimes, I think the bears have the right idea. Wouldn't it be fun to fill our tummies and sleep through the winter? We could have a big family meal, find a nice cozy cave, and hibernate through the blue winter days!

I remember one dreary winter day. Dave called to tell me his current project had just issued him an invitation to a late-night party. He said I should go to bed without him. *Oh,* I thought, *I wish it were already bedtime!* In reality, it was only 4:30 P.M. It

4

was dark outside, and in the house with me were three young boys behaving as if they had just taken double doses of a high-potency vitamin! Suffice it to say that at that moment motherhood was not the exciting experience I had visualized.

I knew it could be a long evening. I also knew that if I could improve my attitude and come up with something positive to do with my three wild Indians, there was still hope for change.

Gathering my tribe, I announced a "Super Winter Surprise." If they wanted to participate in and enjoy the surprise, I told them, I would need their help and cooperation. Their part was to turn down their motors, find their "inside voices," and then take up a quiet activity. Out came one of their favorite cassettes, *The Music Machine*, and along with it a thirty-minute reprieve for me to come up with my "surprise."

Surveying the kitchen, I found three hot dogs and buns, carrots, celery, raisins, bananas, and candy corn left-over from Halloween—everything I needed for a Treasure Hunt Dinner. Already my attitude was changing.

Treasure Hunt Dinner

I divided the food into courses and wrote unpoetic jingles for each course. Here are two examples:

- "The bananas are where the bandanas are found; look in the chest and not on the ground!"
- "Carrots are crunchy and have lots of Vitamin A; search for them where your coats are supposed to stay."

Then I wrapped the different courses of food in plastic bags (if you are concerned about the environment, you might want to put each course in a reusable margarine tub), and hid each in the appropriate place along with the next clue. After courses of carrots, celery, banana, and raisins, the next clue led all three boys to the bathtub for a dip in our "mini-pool."

5

This last maneuver gave me time to warm up the hot dogs and get out the catsup. With bath time now behind us and all three boys in pajamas, Hot Dogs à la Carte were served, accompanied by milk in each boy's favorite cartoon cup. After the dinner feast, one last clue led them to their candy corn dessert. A couple of stories later, all three Indians were bedded down for the evening. What did I do then? I had a wonderful "just-me-and-me" time. I finished my favorite leftovers—and the candy corn—curled up with a good book, and, though exhausted, enjoyed a cozy evening. Amazingly, the winter blues were chased away one more time.

As you think about the coming winter, you too can chase away the winter blues if you are willing to plan ahead. In the following chapters, you are going to find several vehicles. Instead of giving in to the coming winter storms, you can make this winter positive for you and for your family. The approaching winter can be a time of building positive family relationships. The key is preparation. With physical preparation and attitude preparation, you can make this winter a time of change.

Sanity Throughout the Year

More than a decade ago, Linda Dillow and I wrote *Sanity in the Summertime*. Our desire was to share with our readers a new way of relating to their children. In this book, I want to help you consolidate your summer successes. By planning sanity into the coming winter, you can carry over the good times to the rest of the year. You can experience sanity all year long!

Building relationships takes time. No one can tackle a whole year at one time or come up with a detailed plan for the rest of one's life. But we can take winter, break it down into bite-sized pieces, and then come up with a practical plan that will help us enjoy and build up our family.

In *Beating the Winter Blues*, we'll look at those cold dreary months and help you come up with your very own survival plan. What natural opportunities do the winter months offer? Thanksgiving, for instance, is an appropriate time to teach our children to "count their blessings," and at Christmas we can help them discover the joy of giving to others. Easter provides an opportunity to think about God's gift of eternal life and the unique pillars of the Christian faith. What about school days, sick days, snow days, and those "I've-got-nothing-to-do" days? How can we use the coming winter to build relationships with our children?

In the next chapter we will walk through the planning process together. What do you want to accomplish in the next few months? You'll have the opportunity to choose specific goals. You will even find space to map out your winter objectives right in the pages of this book!

Part Two is a guide for building warm relationships with your children in the cold days of winter. Practical activities will help you get to know your children and appreciate their uniqueness. Responsibility developers will help facilitate your children's trip on the road to maturity. And as they mature and want to "break away," we'll look at how we can let go and still be close.

Part Three is full of activities to help make wintertime work for you, while Part Four includes many practical suggestions for celebrating and surviving winter holidays.

A Tribute to MOM's Support Groups

Lest you think that all of the activities in this book are Arp originals, let me clue you in. Although all are tried and tested, there just were not enough growing-up days at the Arp's to do everything. Many of the following activities come from the mothers in MOM's Support Groups, a video-based church and community family enrichment resource that I organized to encourage mothers to enjoy parenting while they live through it!

7

Using videos, study books, exercises, and a comprehensive leader's guide book, groups are easy to start and have spread throughout the United States and Europe.

From these groups come many of the creative ideas in this book. To each parent who contributed, I salute you! The jewels you have passed along will not remain hidden in the pages of an unread book.

Take it from one who knows how fast the years go by—now is the time to enjoy your children and parenting. One mother summed up the urgency of enjoying the present in the following meditation called "Wet Oatmeal Kisses":

> The baby is teething. The children are fighting. Your husband just called and said, "Eat dinner without me." One of these days you'll explode and shout to the kids, "Why don't you grow up and act your age?" And they will.
>
> Or, "You guys get outside and find yourselves something to do. And don't slam that door!" And they don't.
>
> You'll straighten their bedrooms all neat and tidy, tops displayed on the shelf, hangers in the closet, animals caged. You'll yell, "Now I want it to stay this way!" And it will.
>
> You'll yell, "I want complete privacy on the phone. No screaming. Do you hear me?" And no one will answer.
>
> No more plastic tablecloths stained with spaghetti. No more dandelion bouquets. No more iron-on patches. No more wet knotted shoelaces, muddy boots or rubber bands for ponytails.
>
> Imagine—a lipstick with a point, no babysitter for New Year's Eve, washing clothes only once a week. No PTA meeting or silly school plays where your child is a tree. No carpools, blaring stereos, or forgotten lunch money.
>
> No more Christmas presents made of library paste and toothpicks. No wet oatmeal kisses. No more tooth fairy. No more giggles in the dark, scraped knees to kiss, or sticky fingers to clean. Only a voice asking, "Why don't you grow up?" And the silence echoes, "I did."[1]

Author unknown

2

Planning for Wintertime Sanity

It wasn't exactly what you'd call life in the fast lane, but it was close. On Monday, Julie helped in the library at her daughter's school and organized the car pool for her son's basketball league. Tuesday, she was a volunteer for the Crisis Pregnancy Center. Her aerobics Bible study occupied Wednesday mornings. By Wednesday evening, she was bushed as she pulled the last sheet of turkey-shaped cookies (for her child's kindergarten class) out of the oven. As she dusted the flour off her hands, she remembered she still had to prepare for her MOM's Support Group the next day.

Suddenly, tears began to stream down Julie's face. "How did I get into this mess? I've got so much to do and so little time. I want to be a good mother and community leader—but I just can't seem to find the right balance!"

If you identify with Julie, count yourself in the majority of volunteers polled in a 1988 Gallup survey.[1] You want to do something useful and make a difference in your world, so you volunteer to help. But like Julie, you're frustrated when overcommitment sneaks in. You wonder what ever happened to the fun, lazy days of summer?

Moving from the carefree days of summer into the winter months can bring subtle changes in the way we relate to our families. Flexible families become more rigid. The laid-back mom becomes more uptight. Some kids even notice that their parents are different during the school year.

Ten-year-old Jeff put it this way: "Summer is so much fun, and the winter stinks. Mom and Dad play with me and laugh in the summer, but when winter comes, they yell at me to do my school work, and they make me go to my room. I can't concentrate and it stinks."

Enjoyment Preventers

What keeps us from enjoying our children all year round? Think about it. In the summer school doesn't seem to exist. Then, presto—the winter season sneaks in and so do frustrations with homework, grades, sports and all kinds of organized activities. Add dreary, cold winter blue days to the challenge of living in today's pressure-cooker world, and it's no wonder we feel tense and stressed.

When we hurry through life, our relationships tend to suffer. We make comments like "We'll talk about it later"; "Mommy doesn't have time right now"; "Don't ask questions—just do as I say!" Communication breaks down and confusion reigns.

The Hurry Syndrome

One year two of our sons called our cards: "Mom, Dad, you need to slow down. You are both stressed out; there's never a good time to discuss anything. This just isn't like you. You need to get your act together!"

They got our attention, and, sure enough, they were right. We had slipped into the mistake of thinking, *This is temporary; things will slow down tomorrow.* Too often, we hurry through the parenting years, and on the other end find we have missed out on the fun of family life while it was actually happening.

If we are going to achieve balance and beat the blues this winter, we'll have to do some serious evaluation and planning and maybe even make some mid-course changes. So where do we begin?

The Overcommitment Syndrome

The first step of planning for wintertime sanity is to evaluate your current situation. Are you overcommitted? Check any of these symptoms that apply to you:

_____ You're living life faster and enjoying it less.

_____ You haven't had lunch with a friend for months.

_____ Forgetfulness is becoming a way of life. You still haven't found the glasses you lost two months ago!

_____ The laundry you were definitely going to pick up this week got put into summer storage.

_____ You have not signed up for that exercise class.

_____ Once again, last evening you called your kids to dinner by saying, "Children, get in the car!"

You may also be experiencing physical symptoms:

_____ A lingering cold that just won't go away.

_____ A nagging backache that comes and rarely goes.

_____ A low energy level and irritability from skipping meals and poor nutrition.

_____ Lack of regular exercise.

Before we get too exhausted to go on, let's look at how we can fight overcommitment and burnout. Is it really possible to set limits and live by them?

Dr. Herbert Freudenberger, the author (with Gail North) of *Women's Burnout,* stated that mothers of young children are at high risk for overcommitment because of the many demands on their lives. Whether you work outside the home or not, the danger of burnout is both real and serious. Women who must both earn money and raise families are especially vulnerable. "You cannot be perfect in all roles," Freudenberger said. "You have to

11

decide to allow certain things to fall through the cracks or you will fall through."[2]

Look closely at your own lifestyle. What motivates you? Are you trying to please others? Do you have the "savior" complex, in which you think, *If I don't bake those cookies, organize the food drive, or whatever needs to be done, no one else will do it!* Guilt can motivate, and you want to make sure you're not a ready victim.

Smart people build activities around their talents and interests. Obviously, parenting is a major interest or you would not open this book, so here are some tips to work your way out of overcommitment and into a sane winter.

Logging Burnout

Dr. Freudenberger suggests keeping a "Burnout Log" for a period of two weeks.[3] Stop right now, and write down the times you feel the most pressure and stress.

Mom's Burnout Log

The times I feel the most pressure and stress:

1.
2.
3.
4.

Now think about these times. Is anything about them similar? The time of day? The activity? The people who are present? (For example, is there a person or group whose approval you desperately seem to need?) List any similarities you observe.

Similarities I observe:

1.
2.
3.

Maybe you know someone who appears to be so "together" and competent that you're trying to imitate or outdo her performance. One summer when my workload was extra heavy, I decided to forgo planting my vegetable garden. My next-door neighbor, Carol, is an avid gardener and asked to use our garden space. She kept it beautifully groomed, and the vegetables were lush and healthy. She even planted a border of flowers.

I had to chuckle when several friends who were aware of my summer deadlines and projects just couldn't understand how I could be a gardener and writer at the same time! Sometimes (most times), things are not what they seem to be. Don't fall into the trap of comparing yourself with others. If you do, you will be totally frustrated.

We need to realize we can't do it all. We're not bionic and we're not angels who need neither food nor sleep! Before accepting a new responsibility, stop and ask yourself:

- How much will it cost me in time and energy?
- If I accept this new responsibility, can I stop doing something I am presently doing?
- Does this activity advance my personal goals?

Goals—What Are They?

We all would probably agree on certain goals in life: to love and support our mates; to love and nurture our children; to influence our world positively. Most of us are familiar with goal setting, but often our goals are too numerous, too general, or virtually impossible to measure.

One part of the marriage and family enrichment work that Dave and I enjoy doing together is our Marriage Alive Workshop. A vital part of this workshop is helping couples set goals for their marriage. We suggest that their marriage goals meet the following criteria:

- The goal must be specific.
- The goal must be measurable.
- The goal should have a time frame.

For example, a couple may set a goal to spend more time together and work on building a closer relationship with each other. Their actual plan might look something like this:

- We will schedule one date night a week.
- We will walk together for thirty minutes after dinner three times each week.
- We will plan a weekend away alone together in the next two months.
- We will read one book on communication and discuss it within the next month.

Now let's apply the goal-setting principle to our own situation—specifically, this coming winter and our relationship with our children. Our goal is to survive and enjoy the coming winter and to build positive relationships with our children.

To make our goal measurable and specific, we need to come up with our own individual plan. Remember, goal setting is for us—not for our children. Our goals will obviously include things we desire to see happen in the lives of our children, but we need to realize that we can only set goals for ourselves. Otherwise, we are setting ourselves up for failure and frustration.

For example, you might set a goal of helping your children do their best in school this year. As parents, we can do some specific things to give our children the right environment for learning. We can monitor homework time, interact with their teachers, and be available to help, but we cannot take our children's tests, participate in their classes, or write their essays.

Let's go back to Julie. She tried to do it all, but it just didn't work. It wasn't a case of her not caring or being incompetent. To

14

the contrary, she was an overachiever mom. What Julie needed was a large dose of balance. She needed to choose her focus and set her own objectives. After evaluating her own situation, Julie came up with three objectives for her winter:

1. To build positive relationships with her children.
2. To help her children in their school work, sports, and other winter activities.
3. To use the winter holidays in a positive way in her family.

Consider some of the activities Julie chose to do with her children. Then you will have the opportunity to choose your own focus and game plan for your winter.

Objective One: Building Relationships

Julie made a list of special needs for each child. For instance, Jennifer, her five year old, was feeling insecure in her kindergarten class and needed more affirmation and one-to-one time. Julie planned a Just-Me-and-Mom Time into each week for her and Jennifer.

Just-Me-and-Mom Times

Just-Me-and-Mom Times are focused times you spend alone with one child. A Just-Me-and-Mom Time can be as simple as ten minutes of finger play with a toddler on the floor or a planned day or afternoon outing with your ten year old. Younger children love it when you talk about and have Just-Me-and-Mom Times. Older children still need the focused time together, but smart Moms don't call it that! Throughout this book, you will find activities and suggestions for Just-Me-and-Mom Times.

Some of the types of Just-Me-and-Mom Times that Julie planned with daughter Jennifer were stopping off for ice cream and a just-for-two chat on the way home from kindergarten and making muffins together for the evening meal. Sometimes they worked on a simple puzzle or watched an educational video and then talked about what they had seen. Their Just-Me-and-Mom Times were simple, they included one-to-one time together, and most importantly, Julie and Jennifer did them!

Objective Two: Helping with School and Winter Activities

Again Julie made a list for each child. Daughter Megan needed extra help with math—she just couldn't seem to get her multiplication tables down. So Julie spent fifteen minutes a day drilling Megan. To make it fun, she wrote one jingle each day to help Megan remember, like: "Eight times three is twenty-four. Now can you say it before I touch the floor?"

All three children needed some boredom preventers for sick days, snow days, and "I've-got-nothing-to-do" days. One positive action Julie took was to plan and stock a rainy-day chest.

 ## Making a Rainy-Day Chest

Fill a chest or trunk with small, inexpensive games and toys. Wrap each one in Sunday newspaper comics or other colorful paper. Then on rainy days when boredom strikes, open the chest and let each child pick one rainy-day surprise.

Rainy-day surprises don't have to be expensive. As a matter of fact, it's much better if they are not. Here are some suggestions:

Inexpensive books	Paper dolls
Bubble-blowing liquid	Puzzles
Pickup sticks	Simple craft kits.[4]

Julie's plans also included being involved in volunteer work at her children's schools, but to be more selective. The guideline she set was to volunteer no more than two hours per week.

Objective Three: Making Winter Holidays Positive

Julie listed her children's special needs with a reminder to herself not to ignore her family while doing things "for" her family. To help her actually carry through, she made Just-Me-and-Mom coupons for each child.

Just-Me-and-Mom Coupons

To insure that you actually do spend one-to-one time with your children this winter, give each child a Just-Me-and-Mom Coupon Book.

Materials Needed:

Index Cards	Hole puncher	Felt markers
Cute Stickers	Yarn or ribbon	

Instructions: Punch two holes in cards. Decorate cards with stickers. Write out coupons for each child, using one card for one coupon. Tie each child's coupons together with yarn.

Give the coupons to the child at the beginning of winter. Together with your child, schedule times into the winter for each coupon.

Suggested coupons:

Cooking with Mom
Reading with Mom
Shopping with Mom
Playing my favorite game with Mom
Putting together a puzzle (simple) with Mom
A hot chocolate date with Mom[5]

The Just-Me-and-Mom coupons that Julie made for each child were to be cashed between Thanksgiving and Christmas—the most hectic holiday weeks of the year—and were a great way to hold her close to her children at this busy time of year.

Another practical idea that Julie adopted to help her manage the holidays was to list each major winter holiday and choose an emphasis for each. For instance, for Thanksgiving she chose to emphasize being thankful for what they had. The Valentine's Day emphasis was to express love to the extended family by sending homemade valentines with personal notes.

An equally important part of holiday planning was Julie's list of what she was not going to do. It looked something like this:

Things I am not going to do this Christmas:
1. I will not spend money I do not have!
2. I will not take on new commitments for November and December.
3. I will not make a fruitcake since no one likes it but me and I don't need the extra calories!
4. I will not stop my exercise program just because I'm too busy.

Making It Personal

Now look at your winter situation. Using Julie's three general objectives, think about what you can do in each area. By the way, it's okay to write in this book. Remember one way we change is by changing our actions, and one way we act is to write out and plan what we will do. So pull out your pen, and write your intentions right here in your book!

Special Needs Lists

Objective One: Building Positive Relationships
Identify each child's special needs. These might include more time to communicate; a need to feel accepted; more

room to grow, to fail, to develop uniqueness; a need to develop responsibility. Then write your list.

My Child's Special Needs in Our Relationship Are

1.
2.
3.
4.

Objective Two: Helping My Children in School and Other Winter Activities

Consider academic needs, social skills, sports, and other winter activities.

My Child's Special School and Activities Needs Are

1.
2.
3.
4.

Objective Three: Maximizing the Positive Aspects of Winter Holidays with my Children

Consider the need for extra rest, avoiding over stimulation, etc.

My Child's Special Needs During Holidays Are

1.
2.
3.
4.

If you have older children, why not recruit them to help with the planning process? You need all the help you can get and it's a great way to encourage your children to develop responsibility. They will appreciate being a part of the whole planning process. For instance, if your children are involved in planning for Christmas—what you are going to do as well as what you aren't going to do—they are more likely to cooperate!

Mothers Have Needs Too!

It's hard to meet our children's needs if we are needy ourselves. Are you a single parent? Do you work outside the home? Are there too few hours in the day? Are you coping with guilt? (It's a known fact that mothers never "catch up." Therefore we are always behind and are a ready target for guilt.) Are you feeling responsible for things you can't control? What are your special needs?

Mom's Special Needs

Make a list of your special needs and think about how they might be met.

My Special Needs Are
1.
2.
3.
4.

A key to Julie's turnaround was involvement in MOM's Support Group. There she found other mothers who could encourage and support her. Together they worked out their winter plans, and each held the others accountable.

Here's a super winter tip! Consider joining or starting a MOM's Support Group. If there are no MOM's groups in your area, you can write for information about how to start one—possibly through your local church. For more information write to:

MOM's Support Group
P.O. Box 90303
Knoxville, Tennessee 37990

Where to Begin?

The place to begin is where you are. If you discovered this book in September, that's great—you can start planning for wintertime sanity now. If you didn't get this book until January, however, you can still start right where you are. Remember, anytime can be a time of new beginnings—for us and for our children.

Mothers in our MOM's Support Groups have different ages of children from babies to teenagers. One comment we hear over and over is "I wish I had joined MOM's Support Group when my children were younger." But the encouraging message for them and for you, too, is that you can begin at any age to work on improving relationships. So if it's February and you just picked up this book, it's not too late to "beat the winter blues!"

Regardless of our children's ages or the date on the calendar, we can begin afresh to relate, love, nurture, and facilitate our children's lives. Now is the time to begin. So wherever you are, let's get started.

You can't work on everything at the same time—or you will hate me. One mother in Birmingham, Alabama, discovered *Sanity in the Summertime* in April and was elated to have a concrete plan for the coming summer. Being very structured and an overachiever mom, she set rigid goals for each of her three children and then tried to do everything in the book—all in one summer! By the time the end of June rolled around, she was a basket case, and her kids were frustrated. She threw *Sanity in the Summertime* in the garbage and wrote hate letters to Linda and me!

Warning!
Please, oh, please, do not try to do everything in this book in one winter! It is a resource and planning book to help you come up with your own plan and to provide resources for you for many years.

21

Beating the Winter Blues

This book contains one hundred seventy exercises and activities for winter days. They are coded

means the activity is just for mom

activities especially suited for mom and one child

activities for the whole family or mom and one or more children

activities that are super easy

Obviously, you can't do them all. An important part of planning is to plan realistically. Stop right now and evaluate your own situation.

Self-Evaluation

Answer these questions:

1. How many children do you have? ____
   What are their ages? ____
2. What grades are your children in? ____
   Are you home schooling? Yes____ No____
   Do you have preschoolers? Yes____ No____
3. Do you have a supportive partner? Yes____ No____
   Do you parent alone? Yes____ No____
4. Do you work outside the home? Yes____ No____
   Is your schedule flexible? Yes____ No____
   Or is it more rigid? Yes____ No____

5. Do you have a support system? Yes____ No____
   Are you involved in a MOM's Support Group?
   Yes____ No____
   Do you have extended family close by?
   Yes____ No____
6. Do you have good baby sitters? Yes____ No____
   Do you have help in the home? Yes____ No____

Your answers to these questions will help you to determine realistically just how much you can do. For instance if you have three preschoolers and are home schooling your second grader, you will be limited in just how much you can realistically plan and accomplish. Whatever your situation, you need to spend quality time with your children this winter and *Beating the Winter Blues* can help you do just that.

Throughout this book, we call the special one-to-one times Just-Me-and-Mom Times. Many other activities suggested for the whole family are also appropriate for one-to-one times or may be done with more than one child.

Also consider three important times each day you will want to be especially sensitive to your children: at breakfast, after work and school, and at bedtime. Think about what you are presently doing at these important times and also what you would like to start doing.

Now you are ready to plan your program to beat the winter blues.

Plan the Program

Maybe you will want to choose a different emphasis for each month. November could be the month you emphasize really getting to know your children and their unique personalities. December with all the Christmas preparation might be the time to emphasize spiritual growth and thinking about others. January could be the time to work on developing responsibility; February and March, the time to think about helping with decision-making skills and letting go.

After choosing the general emphasis for the specific period of time, list actual activities that you want to do with your children to help you reach your objective. For example:

Objective for November: To get to know my children and strengthen our relationships.

Possible activities:

- Have a Just-Me-and-Mom Time each week with each child.
- Once each week, write a note encouraging each child in a personal area of his or her life.
- Plan a family appreciation night, and establish a family night tradition.

Planning the Program

You will want to do planning for each winter month.
Here's a sample:
Winter Objective for November:

Possible Activities: Estimated time needed:
1.
2.
3.
4.
5.

Plan Your Winter Schedule

Your list of activities may be rather long as you think about all the objectives you want to accomplish. Look at them critically and realistically, and choose those that you most want to do. After all, family life goes on for years, so you don't have to accomplish everything in one winter. On the other hand, if you don't do some strategic planning, you can drift through the parenting years without reaching any of your objectives. So the next step is to schedule chosen activities into your winter.

Planning Your Schedule

You may want to make a chart or calendar for each month. The blank calendar on page 26 is for your use in charting November:

If all this planning seems too time-consuming, you can take a more casual approach to beating the winter blues. As you read through the coming chapters, simply circle the activities that appeal to you. Then decide to do one activity a week with your family.

More Than Blues-Beaters

Remember, you are not just beating the winter blues but facilitating a child's life. Our goal is not just surviving the active parenting years, but building healthy, lasting relationships. What you do in the coming cold days of winter can affect your relationship with your children for years to come. Snow days, sick days, and days when it gets dark oh-so-early, are good times to influence our children's lives.

One huge temptation when your family seems to have too much "wintertime togetherness" is to turn on the television. Stop and think twice before you short-circuit your own winter goals. Woven throughout the following chapters are practical activities and exercises you can do with your children. The resources are here. Your part is to pray, plan, and persevere. Take it from one who knows—it's worth it.

A recent phone conversation with one of our sons corrobo-

NOVEMBER

Sunday	Monday	Tuesday	Wednesday	Thursday	Friday	Saturday

rates this. He was talking about how brave we were to move our family to Austria. "What you did was dangerous," he said. "Raising us in a foreign country had its risks." I had to agree.

"What made the difference?" I asked. "Why do you think it worked out okay for our family?"

After a long pause he responded. "You made it fun. Our family was fun."

Now is the time to consider the coming winter. Now is the time for planning. Now is the time to make it fun!

Part Two

Building
Warm Relationships
in the Mud and Snow

3

To Know Me Is to Love Me

It finally happened—I met a "super mom!" The plane was barely airborne when the mother sitting next to me began to talk about her wonderful relationship with her child! "Our personalities go together like peaches and cream," super mom said. "Since the day my daughter was born," she continued, "I have completely understood her. She is cooperative and has a wonderful easygoing disposition. . . . We just don't have any problems." Of course, her daughter was above average in intelligence and already enrolled in an accelerated learning program. This super mom had read all the books, watched all the parenting videos, and figured everything out. There was only one slight catch—her daughter was only nine months old! I thought silently to myself, "Someday, this baby will grow up. Then super mom had better watch out!"

It's so easy to be an armchair mom and give excellent advice to others. I was a wonderful mother—before I had children. After our boys arrived, motherhood became much more complicated! Dr. Antionette Saunders, a clinical psychologist, said, "I spent twenty years telling people how to raise their kids before I had any of my own." It was much easier for her to come up with creative solutions for her patients. Now that she has a two-year-old daughter, things have changed.

"Last week my two-year-old daughter wanted to wear her bathing suit to preschool," Saunders said. Rather than looking for some deep-seated explanation for her daughter's request or patiently trying to explain to a child who is too young to understand logically why she should not wear a bathing suit to school, Saunders finessed the problem with the wise advice of an experienced parent. She just put the child's regular clothes on over her bathing suit. "It wasn't worth fighting that battle with her," she said.[1]

Kids Come Unique!

It's easy to assume environment has everything to do with how kids turn out—until you look around at kids who grew up in the same home with the same parents and notice that they are total opposites! We are so ready to assign success to parents whose children are friendly, cooperative, and eager to learn. Likewise, we may be critical of those parents whose children are difficult, unhappy, and uncooperative.

Dr. Bonnidell Clouse, author of *Moral Development: Perspectives in Psychology and Christian Belief,* says that characteristics present at birth predispose a child to be active or passive, pleasant or fussy, shy or bold. These inborn personality qualities have been studied by child psychologists and are called temperamental traits; they tend to cluster together into one of four temperament types: "easy," "slow to warm up," "difficult," or "variable."[2]

The Easy Child

As we talk about these four types of children, think of your own kids. Obviously, the super mom on the plane has the easy child, who is generally cheerful and adaptive. Be encouraged. Dr. Clouse says about 40 percent of children fall into this category. Your chances of having at least one easy kid are pretty good! If your child is easy, be thankful, but not proud. Remember your child came that way!

If you have an easy child, it's too easy to let your relationship slide. Because they are easy, they are not demanding, and the more difficult child will tend to get the most attention. To counter this, plan to include the easy child in your normal activities. Why not have a Just-Me-and-Mom-Fixed-It dinner?

Just-Me-and-Mom-Fixed-It Dinner

Together plan a simple menu, and let your child help with the preparation. A fun cookbook for Mom and child is: *Kids Cooking—A Very Slightly Messy Manual* (Klutz Press, 1987). You can order by writing to:

Klutz Press
2121 Staunton Court
Palo Alto, CA 94306

Soups always seem to taste good on cold winter days. If you are really industrious, plan a soup buffet. You can use three or four different soup mixes and let your family pick and choose. Serve with a loaf of homemade bread. I love to use the loaves of dough you can purchase among the frozen foods in grocery stores. All you have to do is let it thaw and rise and then bake. To make the crust thick and crunchy, spray with water a couple of times while the bread is baking.

If you like starting from scratch, consider making this easy soup recipe:

Easy Vegetable Soup[3]

1 pound lean ground beef
1 envelope onion soup
  mix
3 potatoes, cubed

1 10-ounce bag frozen
  peas
1 10-ounce bag frozen
  green beans

33

2 stalks celery	1 10-ounce bag frozen
½ cup barley	corn
1 46-ounce can vegetable	8 cups water
juice	

Directions: Cook ground beef until it crumbles. Drain fat; then put meat in a colander and rinse with hot water to remove any extra fat. Place all ingredients in a 5-quart Dutch oven. Simmer until barley is done. Makes 4 quarts.

Another great quick winter recipe is

Very Quick Spaghetti

Directions: Over medium heat in a heavy pot, add ¼ cup of oil to cover the bottom of the pan and prevent the tomato paste from sticking. Add 2 cans tomato paste to oil and then stir in 1 46-ounce can of tomato juice. Add 3 tablespoons sugar, and salt and pepper to taste. Add bay leaf, oregano, Tabasco—any/all/some/little depending on how spicy you want the sauce. Simmer over low heat up to one hour.

Optional: Lean ground beef may be browned in the pot before you add the tomato paste.

Fry chopped onions until golden in the oil; then add paste.

For table decorations, make place cards with baby pictures of each family member. Each must find his or her own picture.

The Slow-to-Warm-Up Child

Slow-to-warm-up children are not quite as easy. They tend to be more introverted and don't adapt as well as the easy child. This is the kid who has a more difficult time settling into school when she has to go into a totally new situation. To ease school trauma and let your child know you really care, plan a special time to meet your child at school for lunch.

School Lunch Date with Mom

You may want to give your child a written invitation. You could even send it through the mail. Show me a child, and I'll show you someone who enjoys getting personal mail. This activity is great for younger children. Be forewarned: If your child is in middle school or high school, please check first. Chances are he would rather not eat than be caught in the school cafeteria with Mom!

Open-ended Questions

Open-ended questions may work great with your slow-to-warm-up child. While the child may warm up slowly, it's worth the effort to get to know your child. Here are some topics to get you started:

- The funniest thing that ever happened to me . . .
- The place I would like most to visit . . .
- If I had a million dollars, I'd . . .
- What I like best about myself . . .
- What I like best about you . . .
- My best friend is . . .
- My weirdest dream was . . .

The Difficult Child

We all know what we mean when we talk about the "difficult" child. If we don't have one, we know someone who does! As a baby the difficult child was probably very active. Eating and sleeping routines were anything but routine! Difficult babies are chronically cranky and often cry and fuss. This is the child that greets the first day of school each fall with tearful statements like "I hate school!" "I've got a stomach ache and I'm too sick to go to school today!" This child also is usually strong-willed and aggressive. If you have one or more children, you probably feel that you have a difficult child, but Dr. Clouse estimates that only one in ten is truly difficult. It's also relative—whether we are talking about my child or yours!

With the difficult child, it's important to be supportive. Because it is easy to lock horns with difficult children, they need to know they are loved, valued, and accepted—especially by their parents. Just-Me-and-Mom Times are a great way to give focused attention. As you relate one to one with your children to counterbalance their natural negativeness, try teaching them how to give a positive sandwich.

Giving a Positive Sandwich

The difficult child comes with negative feelings. It's okay to express negative feelings, but help the child do it in a positive way. At our house we used "positive sandwiches." The idea is to cushion the negative statement between two positive statements. For example your child might say, "Jay let me play with his Legos, but he called me a nerd. The good news is he didn't hit me!"

Mom could say, "I really appreciate your attempt to clean your room, but clothes under the bed are unacceptable! On the other hand, your desk is well organized. Now what can you do about the clothes?"

With the difficult child, sometimes we communicate better through written notes, so you might write notes to your child.

Note Writing

Writing notes to your child may actually help your child learn to better express his own feelings. Be sure to include lots of positive notes like:

"Your humor is a bright light in our family!"

"This morning was pleasant. Being so cooperative sure made breakfast more pleasant! Keep it up!"

The Variable Child

The variable child is just that—variable! At times he or she will be easy and at other times difficult. Variable children may or may not adjust well to a new situation. Thirty-five percent of children fall into this category.

Remember that these children are variable. At times they love activities—other times they want to be left alone! Your job is to look for open gates.

Finding Open Gates

Watch for times your child appears to be open. Be ready with impromptu activities such as

- Taking a cookie break. Don't just bake cookies. Sit down and eat them together!
- Taking time for a game of Double Solitaire.
- Joining your child in listening to music or watching TV program of his or her choice.
- Making a collage from items found right in your kitchen, like cereal, macaroni, noodles, beans.

Creating a Kitchen Collage[4]

Place all items to be glued in the center of the table. Give each child his own glue. If you can only find one container, squeeze a small amount of glue into a paper cupcake holder or into a piece of foil, and let the child use a toothpick to apply the glue. Give each child a piece of paper, and let him create his masterpiece—perhaps a house with flowers, an animal, or an "original" anything. Display the "masterpieces" and have an impromptu art show.

Variable children need to be built up. They have more potential than others (like teachers) may realize. They need us to believe in them with a constant love and acceptance.

Giving Positive Lunch Notes

Keep cards, stickers, and felt tip pen handy. As our boys were growing up I kept these things in a drawer in the kitchen. Our variable child got a sticker and short note on his napkin in his lunch box each school day. It was simple to do and a fun way to remind him how special he was!

Research reveals that neither the sex of the child nor the order of birth appears to be related to any of the four temperament types. Nor is the disposition of the child correlated with the disposition of the parent.[5]

This is good news for one of our sons, who recently said to us, "I hope we won't have a child just like me!"

One of his brothers commented, "I don't want to have a child like that either!"

Long-term studies show that a child's temperament stays with him or her into adulthood, but environment is still an important factor. By age ten, the way the child is handled in the home is as important as natural temperament!

A fun "how-we-are-different" suggestion is to have a Dinnertime Shuffle.

Dinnertime Shuffle

Let everyone sit in someone else's place at the dinner table and act like that person. Be prepared for an interesting meal! One psychologist who actually did this in his family said he could have written some new case studies with his family as the subjects. He saw himself in a completely different light through the eyes of his ten-year-old daughter, who sat in his place at the dinner table!

Another introspective fun activity is to let each family member evaluate his or her own uniqueness by thinking about "why I'm me."

Why I'm Me

Have family members write descriptions of themselves. Then talk about which are inherited traits and which are acquired traits.

How are you relating to your child? What about the child who is totally different from you? We tend to react to what we don't understand. Or what about the kid who is just like you? There is nothing worse than to see your faults lived out in your child!

It's so easy to react to our children, and before we know it, we hear regrettable statements coming out of our mouths. Wherever there are growing, healthy, and open relationships, there will be transgressions and the need to apologize. In our family we have used a process we call Log Removal.

Log Removal[6]

In Matthew 7:3–5, we read that we are supposed to take the log out of our own eye before we take the speck out of our child's eye. You can accomplish this with a sheet of paper. On the left side of the page, write down whatever is driving you crazy about your child. (*Do not* show this to your child!) On the right side of the page, write down your inappropriate reactions. Did you yell, scream, and explode? That's what you need to deal with.

My log removal page might look like this:

Child's Shortcoming	Mom's Inappropriate Reaction
Left a messy room	• Blew up and called kid a slob living in a pigpen.
	• Compared with "neat" older brother

It is also helpful to add a third column and write how you wish you had reacted. This will help you the next time you face a similar situation. A more appropriate response would be

• After cooling down, write a note requesting child to clean his room.

- At our house, it usually helped to apply humor—like posting a condemned sign on the door. Once I remember sending Joel an invitation to a room cleaning party.
- If humor doesn't work, natural consequences probably will. One mom in a MOM's Support Group gave her teenage daughter this choice: You may go to the ball game with your friends Friday night if your room is cleaned and organized by Friday afternoon.

The next step in log removal is to apologize to your child. It's amazing how forgiving a child can be! I know our sons learned more about keeping relationships healthy through my asking for forgiveness. We learn by repetition, and I was often a model of blowing it! Asking for forgiveness helped to balance things out!

Acceptance Is Vital

You can't really get to know and understand your child unless you are willing to accept her with her corresponding temperament and strengths and weaknesses. Here are three tips.

Thank God for Your Child's Unique Personality

If you have an easy child, be thankful, but also be thankful if you have a strong-willed, aggressive child. Look in the Scriptures. God has often used people with difficult temperaments to do mighty things for His kingdom. I don't think it would have been easy to get along with the apostle Paul!

To get your thoughts going in a positive direction, make a Positive Log Notebook.

Making a Positive Log Notebook

Make or purchase a small notebook for each child. On the first page, write your own description of your child's unique personality. On the second page, list "Unique characteristics my child has for which I am thankful."

Then on the third page, begin a running diary of positive things you observe about your child. Date each entry. You don't have to write something in your notebook each day or even each week, but whenever you observe something special about this child or something really positive, record it. On the days you are ready to resign as resident mom, pull out your Positive Log Notebook and note that tomorrow will probably get better! It will help you keep your perspective!

Along with your Positive Log Notebook, you might start a Prayer Diary for your child.

Making a Prayer Diary

This activity is similar to the Positive Log Notebook. In a notebook, list general things you are praying for your child this winter. On page two start a running diary of prayer requests. Again, you do not have to write something every day. You will know when you feel the need to add an entry— when you are about to start nagging! Allow plenty of space to write in the answered prayer later! I have kept prayer diaries for many years. Now it's fun to read back through them and see just how faithful God is! This activity will encourage you for many winters to come!

One way to appreciate each family member's uniqueness is to have a family appreciation night and talk about how you are different from each other and what you appreciate about each other.

Family Appreciation Night[7]

Give each person a card and pencil. For younger family members who aren't old enough to write, oral answers will be fine. Have each family member write down one thing he or she appreciates about each person in the family. Then take turns in sharing your insights with each other. Two kickoff questions you can use are:

1. What is the greatest strength I bring to our family team?
2. What is the one thing I like best about our family?

You will enjoy hearing the positive answers and your family will be affirmed in the process!

Become a Student of Your Children

Don't assume, just because they are your children, that they will think and act the way you do. Look for the unique characteristics God has placed in their lives and appreciate the difference. If you have a difficult child, don't blame yourself. It doesn't mean you are a bad parent or that you have a bad child. Difficult children did not request that temperamental trait, and growing up will be more stressful for them, so they need your help.

To help your family accept and appreciate your individual uniqueness, why not plan a family puzzle time?

Putting a Puzzle Together as a Family

Try to find a puzzle with diverse people or animals. Once, we put together a puzzle of 501 cats. It was difficult because

43

they were so much alike, but each had unique pieces that only fit one special unique cat!

As you put your puzzle together talk about:

- How we are all unique
- How we fit together as a family
- How each of us is a unique "puzzle"—none of us is "complete"
- The missing pieces and the developing picture. Which do you tend to concentrate on in your family?

A word to the wise: Choose an appropriate level of puzzle. If your children are small, choose an easy one.

Field trips can be fun family times. One family outing that may help you actually understand each other is a trip to the zoo.

Taking a Trip to the Zoo

Take a trip to the zoo. Observe the animals, and talk about how they are different from each other.

If the weather is inclement, go to the library. Look for books with pictures and facts about animals. Talk about the differences among the animals.

Be Patient

You are not looking at a finished puzzle! And you are not producing people—you are facilitating precious lives. Recently someone commented to me, "Claudia, all your boys seemed to peak when they hit college." At times we wondered if our guys would ever peak. Joel was the classic underachiever. We jokingly called him our "closet intellectual" because he hid all academic interest all the way through high school. In college he had to study for the first time and discovered he really liked the academic world. Now one of his favorite activities is reading obscure books he finds in used book stores.

Maybe you have a "late bloomer." Who says the child is late? A culture that dictates designer clothes for toddlers? Your friend, whose child could read at four? The coach, who says kids can never play soccer in high school unless they are in a competitive league by age five? That coach is wrong, and I have the goods to prove it!

I still remember the first time Jarrett and Joel played soccer with their new team in Austria. They were seven and nine. The coach called our home expecting to reach the Paul Stanley family who had previously lived in our apartment. Paul, Jr., played on his team. Now, we aren't talking major competitive soccer. When the coach realized we had two sons of soccer age, he recruited them for the game the next day. He was simply looking for warm bodies.

I'll never forget that game. Joel ran flat-footed—when he ran. He spent most of the game just watching. He was the only spectator on the field. Jarrett couldn't keep his shoelaces tied, and at critical moments he stopped and fiddled with his shoes. The Austrian kids were far more advanced. It wasn't a game to build our boys' parents' self-esteem. Other parents were asking, "Who is number 11, and who is number 16. . . . Why are they just standing there?" The whole experience was enough to make a parent want to go out and buy two oboes.

Even so, both boys went on to play soccer in high school and in college. They didn't develop soccer skills instantaneously or automatically. They worked hard and so did we. One of the nice things about our home in Vienna was that our large "community" backyard was about the size of a soccer field. Even on cold winter days, our boys kicked that soccer ball around and played with friends until it was just too dark to play any more. Then they dragged in, all red-faced, sweaty, and smelling like—well, it was indescribable—but it is etched in my memory bank forever. Our part in helping them develop their soccer skills was pro-

45

viding the "taxi" service to soccer practices and games and encouraging them when they had to "sub" again. (By the way, Joel did learn to run.)

Let me encourage you to begin by seeking to understand and accept the unique children that God has loaned to you for a while. This love and acceptance will translate into caring, close relationships—whether the children are late bloomers, closet intellectuals, variable, or difficult—even if they run flat-footed!

As you learn more about your child's uniqueness, you can begin to relate more positively to that child. Two books that will help you to understand your children's uniqueness are:

1. *How to Really Love Your Child* by Ross Campbell
2. *Key to Your Child's Heart* by Gary Smalley

Put both books on your winter reading list.

Following are some other practical exercises and activities especially designed to help you use this winter to get to know and enjoy your child.

Winter Nature Hike

Bundle up and take a winter nature hike. Even in the cold of winter when most foliage is dead, it's possible to find lovely dried leaves and flowers. And don't overlook evergreens. Talk about what you find:

- How God's colors don't clash
- What kind of leaf you would want to be and why
- What color you would want to be
- How we are all different

Establishing Family Nights[8]

Family Nights are planned times that you are alone together as a family. It is a time to relax and enjoy being together. While Family Night may be an excellent time to work on instilling values and teaching spiritual truths, these will be caught, not taught. Over the years our highest priority was simply to have fun together. The rest just seemed to happen! Here are some guidelines for Family Night:

- Don't overstructure your Family Night. In the winter our children are in school five days a week, and their time at school is very structured. They won't get excited about Family Night if it feels like school.
- Be flexible. You may have chosen your favorite game to play when everyone else is in the mood to read the book you just bought. Relax and trust the group. Go with the flow!
- Consider your objectives—to build strong relationships and strengthen your own family unit and just to have fun!
- Know your family and plan appropriately.
- Relax. Everything doesn't always have to work out perfectly. Just clean up the messes and move on!

Playing Games Together as a Family

Board games to consider are

- The Ungame
- Pictionary

- Balderdash
- Monopoly
- Risk
- Jenga
- Trivial Pursuit (We've just discovered the new Eighties Series, and we even know some of the answers!)

Some card games are

- Double Solitaire
- Go Fishing
- Canasta
- Rook
- Uno

Creating a Self-Esteem Passport for Your Child[9]

Helping your child feel good about himself is not always easy. You might try giving your child a self-esteem passport.

Start by looking at different areas in your child's life. Write down the positive things you see in a "Passport."

- How is your child an original?
- Where has your child recently shown growth? In academics? Relationships? Sports or a hobby?
- How has your child shown personal courage?
- How has your child demonstrated self-confidence?
- Include any other things in your child's life that makes him unique.
- Include your child's picture.
- Let your child decorate the passport with her "original art."

As you spend time with your children this winter, you'll discover all kinds of new things about them. They are wonderfully unique and incredibly complex. You can use winter to renew and strengthen family relationships. Chuck Swindoll says you can't love someone you don't know: "That's basic. . . . You cannot love the unknown. The heart and center of the parent-child relationship is that the parents are engaged in the process of knowing the children God has given them."[10]

Enjoy these fun winter activities. They will help you get to know your child in a more intimate way. To know your child is to love your child!

4

Developing the Big *R*

I was important to the whole operation. My job was complicated. The hours were long, and interpersonal relationships were touchy. I was the shower coordinator!

This situation has a history. When we moved back to the States after living in Austria for years, we were all delighted—especially me—to have more than one bathroom. Winter mornings would be much simpler.

You see, all of us Arps prefer showers, and we all want them in the morning. The "morning" Arps just prefer to start their days that way while the Arp "night owls" use a shower to wake up!

So what's the problem? No problem with our bathrooms. We had plenty of those! The problem was our water heater—our teeny, tiny water heater, of which we have one. Thus my job as shower coordinator emerged.

How did I get involved? I simply wanted to alleviate morning tensions and help everyone get out the door on time. So each night I began negotiations for the next morning. Who had to study late? Who should get up first? Who had a cold? The variables in this operation were many, and I coordinated all of them!

Did it work? You've got to be kidding! On a typical cold winter morning kid number one, who was supposed to be the first in the shower, overslept. Kid number two let the water run too long, so kid number three was frozen and disgruntled and let us all know about it. Happy family? You can forget it!

Finally Dave and I looked at each other and one of us said, "Why are we doing this? The boys are not toddlers. They're in elementary and high school and old enough to work this one out." After all, we agreed, who would coordinate their showers when they were in college or had families of their own? Just whom were we teaching to be responsible, them or us?

You may not be the shower coordinator at your house, but you may find yourself trapped in assuming responsibility for other things—like my friend Cathy who fell into the "potty training trap!" (If you can't remember that one, it's because memory is kind to us and tends to block out the more traumatic events.)

The last time I was with Cathy she was trying to potty train her son, Carter. Things seemed to be going well, so I really chuckled when I received the following letter from her:

"I guess my latest news and triumph is that Carter is now potty trained! I just have to tell you about this—after washing out poopy pants for a couple of weeks when other functions were performed correctly and timely by Carter, I finally told him I was just tired of cleaning up the mess and that he would have to do it by himself.

I closed the door and sat down on the bed and read a magazine—preparing myself for the inevitable mess that I would have to clean up. I really did have to restrain myself when I heard all kinds of noises coming from the bathroom.

"After ample time, I checked on him. He had swished his dirty pants around in the toilet and then filled it up with every scrap of toilet paper we had. Poop was all over him and the floor. I had to bathe him, clean out the toilet, and mop the floor—but guess what? He has not pooped in his pants since then! Poor fellow, I guess he finally smelled it!"

51

We laugh, but seriously, as long as we will clean up their messes, our children will rely on our sense of responsibility and develop none of their own. There is nothing sadder than to see parents of young adults going behind their "children," cleaning up their messes—or coordinating their showers!

Now, back to our shower dilemma. Being the creative geniuses that we are, we bought three alarm clocks and I turned in my resignation as shower coordinator with one brilliant statement: "Kids, you work it out!" Did it work? We had our moments, but now they are young adults, and as far as we know, they are clean ones!

How can we encourage development of responsibility? How can we help our kids clean up their own messes and work out their own problems? The winter months offer lots of "down time." Think about it. It gets darker earlier, forcing our children into their homes earlier. Bad weather days, snow days, sick days—all offer opportunities to tackle a new objective or adopt a new goal. The winter season is a great time to concentrate on helping our children develop more of the big *R*, better known as responsibility.

Qualified and Unemployed

Our goal as parents is to work ourselves out of a job. In fact, one problem with being a parent is that by the time we're really qualified, we're unemployed. What is your goal in parenting?

Authors Jerry and Mary White share their parenting goal in *When Your Kids Aren't Kids Anymore:*

> Our overall goal for our sons and daughters is that they grow into mature, independent, godly adults
>
> who base their lives on sound principles,
> who are emotionally and spiritually strong,
> who have a strong sense of responsibility toward their
>   fellow man,

who will face good and difficult times with calmness
and perseverance, and
who, if married, become competent and faithful husbands,
wives, and parents.[1]

The Whites are quick to add that we parents cannot control the outcome of our young adults' lives, but we can do all we can to influence them!

Take a trip with me to the future. Picture yourself perhaps on a cold winter day when your children—now adults—are all visiting Mom and Dad. What kind of relationships would you like to have with each other at that point? Do you picture lots of laughter and joking? Can you imagine how great it will be to enjoy your adult children without feeling responsible for their lives? If we do an adequate job of teaching responsibility and preparing our children for adulthood, we can look forward to great times together in the future.

While looking at how responsible we want our children to be as adults, let's work backward and see what we need to do to get them there.

What My Child Needs to Know

What do our children need to know by the time they leave home at around the age of eighteen? Will they be able to function as adults? Will they be able to take care of their clothes, manage a checking account, and cook basic meals? Write down what you would like your child to know before he or she leaves the nest.

Let me encourage you to take a couple of minutes right now to write out what you believe your child needs to know or be responsible for at each milestone. This will help you work out your own plan for developing responsibility.

By age eighteen, my child needs to

1.
2.
3.
4.

What do you want when your children enter adolescence? That's about the time they develop a deafness to parental advice. What areas need to be covered before they hit those rocky years?

By the time my child enters adolescence, she needs to

1.
2.
3.
4.

What do we want the children to learn, know, experience by the beginning of middle school? Write this down as well.

When my child enters middle school, he needs to

1.
2.
3.
4.

What should a first grader be prepared for on that first day of school?

My child needs to know the following by the time she begins first grade:

1.
2.
3.
4.

Think about kindergarten? Can your child recite your address and phone number, tie her shoes, discern who to talk to and who to avoid?

By kindergarten, my child needs to

1.
2.
3.
4.

Now that you have some general goals, let's look at this winter and some specific ways we can help our kids develop responsibility. Since it is cold outside, it makes sense to begin right at home.

Research shows that children who help at home learn responsibility, gain self-esteem, and develop valuable work habits for adult life. A recent Harvard Medical School study revealed that those who worked as children, even at simple chores, enjoyed happier and more productive lives than those who had not. They were less likely to be unemployed, were higher paid, and were more likely to have warm relationships with others as adults.[2]

Tap some of your children's endless energy and help them develop responsibility at the same time. The next obvious question is, What are reasonable expectations for different ages and stages? In *Mothers & Sons*, Jean Lush (with Pamela Vredevelt) gives the following breakdown of age-appropriate responsibilities:

Ages Two to Four
1. Pick up toys and put away.
2. Clean up dropped food.
3. Choose between two foods at breakfast. Make simple decisions.
4. Simple hygiene—brush teeth, wash and dry hands and face.

Ages Four to Five
1. Set the table.
2. Put the groceries away.
3. Feed pets on a schedule.
4. Dust the furniture.

Ages Five to Six
1. Help with the meal planning and grocery shopping.
2. Make own sandwich or simple breakfast; then clean up.
3. Prepare the dinner table.
4. Make bed and clean room.

First Grade
1. Choose clothing for the day.
2. Water plants and flowers.
3. Cook simple foods (hot dogs, boiled eggs, and toast with assistance).
4. Rake leaves and weeds.

Second Grade
1. Oil and care for bike.
2. Take phone messages.
3. Water the lawn.
4. Wash dog or cat.

Third Grade
1. Fold napkins properly and set silverware properly.
2. Straighten closet and drawers.
3. Shop for and select own clothing with parents.
4. Begin to read recipes and cook for the family.

Fourth Grade
1. Operate washer and dryer.
2. Prepare a simple family meal.
3. Receive and answer own mail.
4. Wait on guest.

Fifth Grade
1. Be alone at home for short periods.
2. Handle sums of money up to $5.
2. Take the city bus.
4. Responsible for personal hobby.

Sixth Grade
1. Join outside organizations, do assignments, and attend.
2. Put siblings to bed and dress them.

3. Mow lawn with supervision.
4. Schedule time for studies.[3]

Unless you have a full house of easy, cooperative children, just knowing what responsibilities are appropriate for what ages won't produce much activity. How can we make chores fun? Sharon Johnson, who speaks on the subject of time management, has these suggestions:

Playing The President Is Coming!

Make helping a game. Play "The President Is Coming!" when you need extra help in tidying up the house quickly.

Beat the Clock

Set the timer for fifteen minutes and play Beat the Clock. See if the children can complete their jobs before the buzzer rings.

A Zone Offense

Divide the house into zones, with each family member keeping an area clean. Then have a contest and give rewards for the person with the cleanest zone.

The Job Jar

Have a job jar. Write each chore on a slip of paper, place it in the job jar, and have each person draw for this task. For difficult tasks, assign job teams.[4]

Before you can expect children to pick up, you must teach them how. A fun game to do this is Do You Live Here?

Do You Live Here?

With your young child, walk up to something in the room and say "Do you live here?" Then pretend that the object you have addressed answers you. For example, you could say to the coffee table, "Coffee table, do you live here?" The coffee table answers, "Yes." Then ask the ball on the floor by the table, "Ball, do you live here?" Let your child answer for the ball, "No, I don't live here. I live in the toy box." Then, let the child take the ball to its home, the toy box. Continue the game as long as your child will participate and it's fun.

A variation of the Do-You-Live-Here? game is to use sounds or letters of the alphabet. "Can you find something that needs to be picked up that begins with a *B* sound?" Your child might find the book on the couch that needs to be returned to the bookshelf. Another optional pick-up activity is to let your child find two things on the floor that don't belong there or two things on the table that need to be put away.

Many other tactics have been used to motivate children to help around the house, but most do not work. At the top of the list may be charts!

Charting It Out

Charts can let children know what is expected of them and help parents to follow through. The secret of using charts effectively is changing and switching them. Consider weekly charts, one-time charts, or perhaps even a morning checklist.

Morning Chart

Before I leave for school this morning I will

_____ Get up on time on my own.
_____ Get dressed.
_____ Make my bed.
_____ Eat a healthy breakfast.
_____ Brush my teeth.
_____ Comb my hair.

A book to add to your winter reading list is *The Big R: Responsibility* by Gene Bedley. As a father of three and a school principal, he knows what he's talking about. He says, "What really serves children is helping them understand how to respond to the world. Responsibility can be simply defined as my ability to respond. Encouraging responsibility amounts to helping a child see cause and effect. The bottom line of what responsibility means is this: I come to a place in my life where I acknowledge what I do."[5]

Establishing guidelines can help children do just that.

Establishing House Rules

One friend has the following plaque on her refrigerator to remind her children that she is helping them develop responsibility!

House Rules

When I turn it on . . .	I turn it off.
When I unlock something . . .	I lock it up.
When I drop something . . .	I pick it up.
When I break something . . .	I repair it.
When I open something . . .	I close it.
When I make a mess . . .	I clean it up.
When I make a promise . . .	I keep my promise.
When I find something . . .	I return it.
When I borrow something . . .	I give it back.
When I take it out . . .	I put it back.
When I am assigned a task . . .	I complete it on time.
When I earn money . . .	I spend and invest it wisely.[6]

An old Chinese proverb goes something like this: "To manage money, you have to have some money!" To that we add the Arp proverb: "To have some money, you have to earn some money!" This thought motivated our three boys to begin their very first business venture. Peanut butter was not readily available in Austria. Peanuts weren't that expensive to buy, so our three sons began their peanut butter business as the Arp Peanut Brothers.

Learning to Manage Money

This business was a partnership, so all three boys had to come up with a business plan and basic operating procedures. They based individual income on time invested in making peanut butter. They kept books and records of time spent making peanut butter and the number of jars sold. Each month they received their share of the profits. They made their own labels and had their own motto: "You can trust us; we're all nuts for you!" The Arp Peanut Brothers' business venture proved to be an excellent way for them to develop responsibility and to see the benefits of hard work. One month one of the boys earned only fifteen cents while his two brothers earned twelve dollars and five dollars. The next month he really got with it and did his share of the work—and earned his share of the profits!

Please note. This business operated out of my kitchen! Need I say more? There is a reason not one set of parents in Vienna, Austria, wanted their children to assume the peanut butter business when we moved back to the States. When we encourage our children to get involved in businesses and other activities that help them develop responsibility, many times—most of the time—it requires extra patience and commitment from us. But Dave and I were convinced that children need working experiences to help them develop responsibility.

Developing a peanut butter business isn't that practical in the peanut butter capital of the world where nuts are more expensive than peanut butter. What can kids do in the wintertime to earn money? Consider the following:

Money Earning Suggestions

Consider these fun ways for your kids to earn money:

- Pet sitting
- Dog walking
- Baby sitting
- Reading to senior citizens
- Assisting at parties
- Emptying trash
- Cleaning and organizing attics and garages
- Cleaning our crawl spaces and storage sheds
- Simple home maintenance projects
- House sitting
- Gofering
- Typing and word processing
- Letter writing for elderly people
- Selling toys (children's version of a garage sale)

- Making and selling Christmas tree decorations
- Making and selling Christmas wreaths
- Delivering papers.

Once our children earn money, then what? How can we use the winter months to teach good money management? In today's world, who is a reliable teacher about money management? Can you trust your banker? Your stock broker? The financial pages of the evening paper? The tip from your neighbor? The safest and best information source that we have found for wise money management principles is the Scriptures. The Bible has lots to say about money. Let's consider four facets of managing money: earning, giving, saving, and spending.

 Family Financial Bible Study

For a fun Family Night activity, look up verses on earning, giving, saving, and spending, and discuss them with your family. The way you approach this study will depend on the ages of your children and your family style. Consider the following:

- Choose one topic, and use this study for four sessions.
- Ask questions to make the verses personal:
  - What does this verse say to me?
  - How does this verse relate to our family?
  - What changes do I need to make in my own life?
- Write out verses on small pieces of paper and put them in a hat or a jar. Take turns drawing out one verse at a time. Identify whether the verse deals with earning, giving, saving, or spending.
- Talk about people you know who have real needs and what your family can do to help.
- Choose a family project that includes earning, giving, saving, and spending. For example, you could plan a

family garage sale. From the amount of money earned, decide how much you want to save, to whom and how much you want to give, and one special thing you would like to do as a family or purchase for your family.

Following are several verses to get you started. Use a concordance or cross-references to find other verses on these four important subjects.

EARN:

Proverbs 14:23
Proverbs 20:4
Proverbs 24:30–34
Proverbs 21:5

GIVE

Proverbs 3:9–10
2 Corinthians 9:7–14
Proverbs 28:27
Philippians 4:10, 16, 18–19
Luke 6:38
2 Corinthians 9:6
Proverbs 19:17

SAVE:

Proverbs 16:8
Proverbs 22:7
Proverbs 23:4–5
Proverbs 16:1
Proverbs 30:25

SPEND:

Proverbs 30:8–9
Psalm 37:16
Matthew 6:25–34
Philippians 4:11–14

Playing Give, Earn, Save, Spend Game

Write the words, *Give, Earn, Save,* and *Spend* on separate index cards for each family member.

Take turns making up situations that could involve giving, earning, saving, or spending. Then read one statement at a time to the rest of the family.

After a statement is read, have each person hold up a card that indicates what his or her initial reaction to the situation would be. Discuss your responses. What are the advantages of giving, earning, saving, or spending in each situation?

Examples of statements you might use are:

- "You received a gift of ten dollars from your grandparents for Christmas."
- "Your best friend's birthday is next week."
- "Your church is putting together food baskets for needy families for Thanksgiving."
- "The ball game is next Friday night."
- "You received five requests for donation in the mail today."
- "You earned ten dollars cleaning out the garage."

Another fun activity to emphasize planning and saving is to observe our small friends, the ants.

Looking at the Ants!

How do the ants ever do it?

Have you ever watched ants carry tiny bits of food? Where do the ants take the food? What do they eat in the winter when it's cold and they can't find food?

Read Proverbs 30:25 in the Living Bible. Use felt pens to make posters of ants. Write the Bible verse on it. Or make your own paraphrase: "Remember the ants—save a dime for later."

To actually see some ants at work, you may want to purchase an ant farm from your hobby store.[7]

Once your children have learned the delayed gratification of saving, they will need a place to keep their coins. Why not make a tub bank?

Easy-to-Make Banks

Cut a slit in the lid of a margerine tub. Let your child decorate the tub with stickers, self-adhesive vinyl, or permanent-ink felt pens. This is an easy-to-make bank for your child's weekly savings.

Parents' Checklist

To test your effectiveness in helping your older children develop financial responsibility, consider this checklist. Put a check by the things your child already does.

Parents' Checklist for Older Children

Does your child/teenager know how to:

_____ Tithe, save, and spend on an allowance budget?

_____ Earn extra money for special projects?

_____ Write a check?

_____ Explain how interest accrues in an account?

_____ Deposit money in a savings or bank account?

_____ Understand how you earn money?

_____ Understand how your family pays bills? Tithes? Pays for food, housing, etc.?

_____ Buy quality sale items?

_____ Share her own possessions with those in special need?

A great way to help your children develop responsibility is to introduce the tradition of Family Conferences.

Begin Family Conferences

Family conferences can make family planning and decision making a lot more fun at your house. Listen to one mom's experience: "We started family conferences when our older child was seven and our younger was three. Even at those young ages, the children enjoyed them, respected the decisions that came out of them, and learned the basics of leading a meeting in a fun way."

Family Conferences

Rules for this family's conferences are simple:

1. Anyone can call a family conference, but adequate no-

tice must be given. No one is forced to cancel previously made plans.

2. All family members must be present to have a family meeting.
3. The agenda is open. Each person has a chance to bring up anything he or she wants to talk about, whether action is needed on it or not. No new topic can be brought up until the one being discussed is completed.
4. The leader for the family meeting rotates. Minutes are kept so that what is decided and who leads the meeting is not in question. In our house, Mom keeps the minutes.
5. Parents have the right to say that a topic may be discussed but is not open to a vote. (This comes in handy when children want to discuss chores repeatedly and want to vote that they don't have to do any.)
6. Each person has one vote. Majority rules. Ties mean no action—nothing changes. If the children outnumber the parents, don't worry. You just have to be careful to not let things that would harm the family come to a vote. For example, you can discuss which child does what chores but not vote on whether or not the chores can be transferred to the parents.
7. Each person must vote what he or she thinks is best, not what someone else might want them to vote. In other words, vote your heart. No deal making. That's called political purity.

Don't overdo the family meetings, and keep the agendas short. Sometimes that's not possible because the children will keep it going. As long as they are interested, that's fine. Just make sure that the parental contributions don't go on and on.

You may be thinking, "My children are so young, they are years away from starting a business, opening a checking account, or leading a family conference. This section just doesn't apply to my family situation." Don't be so quick to count yourself out. Your child develops responsibility by being accountable for his or her actions. Even very young children can begin to make choices and little decisions. If your child makes a mess, let him clean it up. It may be easier to pick up the toys yourself—or whatever the current chore is, but it's better to let your child have the experience of doing it.

We recently visited friends who have three boys—very young boys, ages four and under. It was right before Christmas, and our friends had tapped their sons' toddler power to help decorate the Christmas tree. How did we know? It was obvious. All the candy canes were bunched on one limb on the tree. This particular limb was low and easy for little hands to reach. Now I know Dan and Leah could have done a much better job of distributing the candy canes and of decorating the tree in general—but they laughed along with us. You see, they are helping their boys on the road to maturity, not striving for the perfect tree. And from our observations, they're doing a great job of growing healthy boys! (If you are a compulsive perfectionist, consider having two Christmas trees, but hands off the kiddie tree!)

Wherever you are in your family life, whatever the ages of your children, remember our goal in developing the big R is to raise our children to become independent contributing adults. We are working ourselves out of a job and into a life-long relationship to be cherished and enjoyed. In the meantime, wouldn't it be great to occasionally hear on a cold winter day, "Hey, Mom, is there something I can do to help you?"

5

Breaking Away and Letting Go

It had been a long, cold Austrian winter, so naturally we were excited when friends offered us their chalet in Aldelboden, Switzerland, for a weekend family getaway. Just thinking about a weekend away in the Swiss Alps filled us all with warm thoughts. It sounded relaxing—even with our three boys, ages three, six, and eight.

I was prepared. I had cooked food for the weekend and had packed for all five of us. The car trip produced no disasters—just the normal "I want to sit by the window. . . . I'm hungry. . . . I need to go to the bathroom. . . . How much longer till we're there?" Our standard answer, "Not over five hours," didn't seem to satisfy.

The first Saturday morning at the chalet began early—much too early for a Saturday morning! Dave and I quickly remembered the benefits of a weekend away alone without the children! But this was not to be one of those.

The cereal boxes came out. Why do advertisers try to sell us cereal guaranteed to give children energy? With our active tribe, I would have preferred a cereal that zaps a kid's energy!

All three boys filled their "tiger tanks" and were ready to go. We were all looking forward to our major activity of the day—a long hike in the beautiful Swiss Alps.

All those storybook pictures of Switzerland are true. It was breathtaking (in more ways than one). Picture majestic snow-covered mountains on both sides of a narrow valley. The walking path wove through the towering trees. The first signs of spring were peeping up through the melting snow.

It was quiet. No televisions or stereos were blaring. No cars or trains rushed by—just a wonderful silence, accented of course by three very vocal young boys. Then we heard a noise, a rumbling noise—but it wasn't thunder! It was an avalanche!

Fear gripped my heart. I had heard many stories about avalanches, but this was my first encounter with one. We immediately swung into action. Dave grabbed Jonathan, our three-year-old, and we began to climb up as fast as we could to higher ground.

If the avalanche was on our side, it wouldn't really help. We'd just be buried in snow a little higher. But it was one of those times when you have to do something. With great relief, we saw tons of snow rolling down the mountain across the valley.

Parenting sometimes is like our "avalanche experience." Do you ever feel your children are breaking away like the snow in an avalanche, and you're losing control? Sometimes it seems our kids are an avalanche waiting to happen, and we parents get buried in their drive for independence.

Programed for Independence

Amazingly, God has genetically programed each of our children to achieve independence. Fortunately, parents do not need to teach physical developmental skills. That follows a predictable order, but each child will have his or her own timetable.

Just as babies and toddlers develop on their own time schedule, we need to give our older children similar freedom to be unique in their development. It's helpful to realize that, as parents, we cannot (or would not want to) completely control their developmental process. As our children reach the early adolescent years, they not only develop in stages, but they may appear adult one day and out of control, like an avalanche, the next day. How can we deal with their ups and downs and at the same time guide them into maturity?

Avalanche Alert

We all experience the daily breaking away. These little "mini-avalanches" are sometimes scary, sometimes uncomfortable, but usually manageable. It's the big avalanches that are petrifying—the events that strike with no warning and leave us feeling totally out of control.

In times like these, it's important to realize that our self-worth is not dependent on how our children behave or what decisions they make or don't make. We all know children who grew up in unbelievably negative situations, yet as adults they appear miraculously to have it all together. On the other hand, we know of parents who gave parenting their best shot, yet one or more of their children seems to be really out in left field.

So when you are in the avalanche season at your house, don't take all the blame, and when things are going smoothly, be thankful, but don't take all the credit!

Avalanche Survey

Take a couple of minutes to identify avalanche situations at your house. List recent mini-avalanches, the minor issues that seem to arise daily: unmade beds, toys not put away, homework done messily or not at all, weirdly styled hair (your kid thinks it's great).

Mini-avalanches recently appearing in my home were:

71

1.
2.
3.
4.

Now list any big avalanches like talking back disrespect-fully, deception, lying and half-truths, the cigarettes found on the couch, and the beer bottle found buried in the trash can. You also may want to list ones that might be impending.

1.
2.
3.
4.

Diffusing Avalanches

In Switzerland late winter is avalanche time. Avalanches tend to occur when the temperature warms up, right after a big, heavy snow.

There are scientists who study avalanches and determine where they are most likely to occur. Then, before the snow becomes too heavy, they engineer little explosions all along to keep the snow from building up to dangerous levels.

Like the avalanche observers, we parents can do some things to diffuse and cushion the breaking away process. Remember, our children must separate themselves from us if they are to become mature adults. The breaking away is necessary and healthy. It helps them achieve independence.

We want to lose control, but in a controlled way. In the last chapter we concentrated on helping our children develop responsibility. Helping them to make appropriate choices and wise decisions enables them to break away.

Four Suggestions

Following are four suggestions to make our jobs easier:

72

1. We need to develop an effective communication system.
2. We need to teach our children to set personal goals.
3. We need a plan of release.
4. We need to grow individually.

Communicating Effectively

The effectiveness of our communication with our child says a lot about the depth of our relationship with that child. Parents naturally want close relationships with their children, and that includes one with good communication. Communication, a two-way street, starts with our ability to listen. As if we were tossing a ball, we must "catch" what our children are trying to say to us and understand the feelings behind the words.

Too often we are guilty of selective listening. We do not want to hear our child's feelings about quitting gymnastics or hating math! However, we can listen without approving of their behavior or agreeing with their perspective. At times, our children simply need us to hear them out.

How to Get a Kid to Talk

Listening is one sure way to get your kid to talk to you. When we listen with interest, our children feel that their ideas are valued and that they are respected. This gives the child a sense of self-esteem and confidence. The child reasons, "If my parents believe I'm worth listening to, I must be a person of value and importance." When our children feel good about who they are, we may find that the avalanches that come our way are small.

Six Avalanche Reducers

Here are six avalanche reducers to help improve communication at your house:

1. Be attentive when your child wants to talk with you. Stop what you're doing as soon as you can and give full attention. Put down the paper, turn off the water, and focus on your child. Remember the importance of eye contact. Be sensitive to the tone of voice and facial expression. Let your nonverbal cues tell your child you are available. Really work at understanding what your child is really trying to say to you by completing the communication circle.

Completing the Communication Circle

The first person makes a statement. The second person says, "What I hear you saying is . . ." and then interprets what the first person said. The first person then affirms the interpretation or repeats the statement. Continue until both of you are getting the same message and understand what the other person is actually saying. The goal is understanding what the other is saying, not necessarily agreeing or putting words in the other person's mouth.

---

2. Encourage talk. Smiles, nods, and one-word responses indicate interest. Keep questions brief, open, and friendly; and try to avoid asking "why" questions. When your child's favorite responses are one-syllable grunts or words like "Nope," "Un-huh," or "Yep," try playing Communication Tennis.

Communication Tennis

With a tennis ball in hand make a statement or ask a question that requires a response. At the same time pitch the tennis ball to your child. He answers your question and then makes a statement or asks a question that requires you to respond and pitches the ball back to you. See how long you can keep passing the ball back and forth. This is a good way to help children learn to initiate conversations with grandparents, relatives, or other adults with whom they have difficulty carrying on a conversation.

---

3. Empathize with your child. Acknowledge your child's feelings to encourage her to continue talking about them. Try to put yourself into her shoes. Now this may take imagination and patience, but it will help you understand your child's actions and reactions much better if you will try to identify her feelings.

 Identifying Feelings

Identify feelings as your child exhibits them: "You must feel proud of yourself for finishing that puzzle."

Look for five opportunities to identify with your child's feelings. You might say, "Bet you are disappointed that your friend can't play with you this afternoon," or "You must feel great that your homework is all completed and you can go out to play."

---

4. Listen with respect. Try to react to your child as you would to an adult friend. Listen as much as you talk. Face the fact that at times kids are complainers. Let them get their grievances off their chests. Hear them out. This is not a game of Jeopardy where you are racing to get the right answer! Save any advice for the end of the conversation. Sometimes your child is only asking you to listen and understand how he feels.

Talk, Don't Bug!

What's the difference in talking and bugging? According to one of our sons, talking is when you don't want anything and you communicate. Bugging is when you talk in order to get your kid to do something. For the next twenty-four hours, see how much talking you do without bugging. That means no advice or subtle manipulation! Try it. It's not easy!

5. *Help your child identify her feelings.* As we attune ourselves to our children and reflect feelings back to them, we help them build a healthy self-concept that will equip them for life, for breaking away and letting go. Preschool and early elementary age children may enjoy playing Name That Feeling.

Naming That Feeling

Take turns identifying facial expressions. You can make a face and let your child describe it as "an angry look" or "a happy look." You can also look through a magazine and identify feelings of the people you see in the pictures.[1]

Playing Tell Me About . . ."

Discuss something that

- Was funny
- Embarrassed you

- Was weird
- Made you feel proud
- _____ (make up your own!)

You may want to tell your child about things that happened when you were their age. They are always amazed that you may have been embarrassed or made your mother angry.

---

6. *If you are having difficulty communicating with your child, step back and pretend he is someone else's child.* It will help you see your child in a whole new light. We are usually more understanding with other people's children than we are with our own!

A large part of a child's self-concept emerges from the way he thinks his parents see him. When children are loved, listened to, and respected by their parents, they are inclined to accept their own worth as people.

More Communication Builders

Here are other communication activities that you can use on cold winter days (or any days):

Adopting a Puppet[2]

If you want to add to your family communication, consider adopting a family puppet. Puppets are great for younger children who—because of embarrassment, shyness, stubbornness, or whatever reason—will not open up. It is easier for them to express themselves through a puppet than to tell you things face to face.

You can choose from lots of cute puppets in your local toy store, or you can make your own out of fingers of old rubber gloves, socks, or sacks. To get conversations going with your child and your new puppet friend, use open-ended statements like:

- If I had three wishes, I'd wish for . . .
- The thing I like most about my family is . . .
- When I grow up, I'd like to . . .
- If I were a parent, I would . . .
- What I like best about myself is . . .

Creating a Communication Center

Do you have a communication center in your home? You can use a chalkboard, bulletin board, or refrigerator door (our favorite). The key is to put the center where everyone will see it and use it.

You can turn your refrigerator into a communication center with some magnets, note pads, and a little creativity. What goes on the refrigerator? Anything and everything.

- Notes and messages
- Special snapshots and memories
- Cartoons and jokes
- Special proverbs, verses, and sayings
- Newspaper clippings
- Report cards or newspaper clippings that praise your child
- Any other message that is of interest to your family

Helping Our Children Set Personal Goals

One helpful tool for teaching goal setting is to give your children challenges, and wintertime is a great time to use this strategy. A challenge may be worked out cooperatively between parent and child. It needs to be achievable and measurable and may include a celebration or reward at completion. Keep it simple and under two or three weeks at first.

Adopting a Preschool Challenge

A preschooler may learn

- Child and parent's full name
- Address
- Phone number
- ABC's
- Basic numbers
- Colors

As you adopt a preschool challenge, let me challenge you to make it fun and not push your child to excel. Pushing only adds to a child's stress level, and stress is one thing we all can do with less of! For instance, let's take the challenge of learning colors. Why not plan a Just-Me-and-Mom field trip to a craft or fabric store. Usually you can purchase small inexpen-

79

sive squares of felt in many bright colors. Let your child pick colors she doesn't recognize the names for. Later, at home, talk about the names of the colors. You may even want to write the name of each color right on the felt sample. Use a broad-tipped felt marker. After all these colors are mastered, you can repeat the activity.

Adopting an Elementary School Challenge

The mother of an elementary school child might help him or her plan one of the following challenges:

- Read a book of his or her choice and write a book report.
- Learn how to sort the dirty clothes and operate the washer and dryer.
- Select eight or ten key Bible verses and memorize them.
- Learn to use a word processor.
- Begin keeping a journal that could be organized in a notebook.
- Read the Bible daily; put a star or check on the calendar each day the Bible reading is completed. Try to read six days each week; reward biweekly.
- Make a salad or dessert for dinner once a week for three weeks.
- Adopt a shut-in from church and visit once a week.
- Keep a diary of a special trip or school vacation.

For example, we spent one Christmas when Jonathan was in the early elementary years in the United States. Before we left Austria for America, we challenged Jonathan to keep a diary of his trip. Each day he made an entry. Sometimes it was a whole paragraph; other days he drew pictures of airplanes, houses, the ocean, Grandmother, Grandfather, and other relatives he visited. Years later, it's a reminder of a challenge that was positive fun and helped to fill the hours on planes and in cars and at less than interesting places he found himself.

You can find other challenge suggestions in *Sanity in the Summertime* and *Almost 13* (Nashville: Thomas Nelson).

Developing a Plan of Release

Just as scientists plan for facilitating the release of avalanches, we need to have our own plan for facilitating our children's release into adulthood. If the ultimate goal of parenting is to prepare our children to function independently, then we need to begin early to plan for the actual launching from the home pad.

Looking Toward the Adolescent Years

Just the thought of releasing decision making into the hand of an adolescent can strike terror in the heart of any parent. You might use the winter months to plan and execute a Teenage Challenge. Listen to the comments of one mother who did: "My daughter is now twenty-one. Several months before her thirteenth birthday, we planned and implemented her teenage challenge. That time we invested is one of her (and my) fondest memories, and she actually used some of the activities from her teenage challenge in her college admissions essays!"

The Teenage Challenge[3]

A practical tool called the Teenage Challenge is a one-time project to help our children prepare for and make the transition to the teen years. Basically we want to help our preteens

81

feel capable, and we can do this by helping them check off a list of tasks showing that they are able to handle adult jobs. Our desire is to give them a chance to succeed with real-world skills.

The challenge includes achievement in four different areas: physical, mental, spiritual, and practical. An important message accompanies this proposal: "We are excited that you are growing up. You're on your way to adulthood. We want you to be ready for this new phase of your life, and this challenge will help you to prepare. It is a big deal! You are going to be a teenager. As your parents, we are happy about this!"

The Teenage Challenge can be done anytime during the year. Consider challenging your soon-to-be teen this winter. Here are the steps to develop a Teenage Challenge:

1. List positive areas you would like to reinforce (special talents such as sports, music, and art; good study habits).

 1.
 2.
 3.

2. List areas you would like to strengthen (decision making, money management, and time management).

 1.
 2.
 3.

3. From the two lists write specific goals:

• Physical goals (run a mile in eight minutes, or walk four miles in sixty minutes, or begin an exercise program, or learn a new sport)

• Mental goals (reading a biography of some great person in history and writing a report or researching possible professions)

• Spiritual goals (memorizing a chapter in the Bible; or

doing a topical Bible study about youth, faith, truthful-
ness, or faithfulness; or starting a prayer diary)

- Practical Goals (earning and saving fifty dollars or preparing family dinners for a week).

4. Evaluate the challenge by answering these questions:
- Is it practical? Have I included too much or too little?
- Is it programmed for success?
- Is it measurable?
- Are the rewards clearly defined?

Your soon-to-be teenager may be excited about having a
Teenage Challenge. Two of our sons were, but the other
needed some external motivation. So together we chose an
appropriate reward toward which he wanted to work. The reward could be anything from a camera to a new outfit that the
new teen gets to choose on her own.

Setting specific times to evaluate how your young adolescent
is doing will help monitor progress. When the challenge is finished, be sure to celebrate. We gave each of our sons a Certificate of Teenagehood that was framed and hung on their
walls—at least for a while! One message must come through:
"You are growing up and we are excited about it!"

Growing as a Person

We can get too caught up with our children. Their problems
can seem so all-encompassing that we forget that we have lives
too!

An important part of the releasing process is to evaluate your
own life and look for ways you want to grow. What are you doing
to build your marriage? Remember, when you start releasing
your children into adulthood, the empty nest is coming up soon.
Will you be in it with your best friend?

If you are a single mom, you may need to stop for a minute and ask yourself, "Just what are my needs?" Carrying the responsibility of parenthood alone can often cause you to suppress your own desires. If you find yourself in this situation, one possible solution is to assess and possibly expand your resources. Perhaps your extended family can support you more in your parenting role. What about community and church resources?

Make a list of things you would like to do personally this winter to grow. Maybe you want to take a course, start a hobby, or learn a new sport. It might be as simple as figuring out how you can get more sleep at night. (On second thought, that one might not be that simple, but it might be a worthy goal to go for!)

Ways I Want to Grow this Winter

1.

2.

3.

A last tip in the releasing department is to develop a sense of humor. Laughing at ourselves is a great relaxation aid. If joking comes naturally in your home, you're fortunate. Some families are natural cutups while others have to work to keep the atmosphere light. Cruel, hurtful, angry voices can cause avalanches in our homes, but laughter, words of affirmation, and encouragement are noises that will help prevent some from occurring and will cushion the others.

Now let's move on to more avalanche preventers. Let's talk about making wintertime activities like school and sports work for us!

Part Three

Making Winter Activities
Work for You

6

Schooltime Sanity Savers

I am well educated. I've been all the way through school almost four times! I'll never forget a conversation I had with Jonathan when he began high school. He is our "variable" kid, and variable translates into parent panic when it comes to school and academics. After all, doesn't the word *consistency* (the opposite of variable) rank somewhere next to cleanliness?

"Jonathan," I bravely began, "I've been through high school three times. I went to high school myself years ago. I went all the way through high school with Jarrett, and I graduated from high school last year with Joel."

"I just want you to know," I continued, "I won't be going to high school with you. I know you will do well, but you'll have to go it alone. I'm finished with high school!"

His puzzled expression seemed to say, "Gee, Mom, that's a relief!"

A relief for him, but hard for me. It was hard for me to see poor time management, papers thrown together the night before they were due, or papers forgotten altogether! Can you identify with me?

Tips for Schooltime Sanity

Recently I saw a bumper sticker that said, "My child is on the Honor Roll at Ball Camp School." I've never seen a bumper sticker that said, "My child is a *C* student at Podunk High." We are told that C is average, but no one wants their child to be an average student! Yet someone realistically observed that God must really love average people because He made so many of them.

I remember well the first report card in the Arp house. My oldest son, Jarrett, came home with straight C's—not exactly what this overachiever mom was expecting! To this day, I believe God gave me the appropriate response—"Why, Jarrett, that's a wonderful report card—you're passing everything. But there is still room for improvement!"

Maybe you have a houseful of kids who have room for academic improvement. Blended in with the average students are the underachievers and the overachievers. I don't know which is worst.

The underachiever kids drive you crazy because you see so much unused potential! On the other extreme is the kid whose perceived personal worth is so tied to his school performance that he develops an ulcer.

Many children look forward to school. Others bury their heads in Mom's skirt leaving wet spots from tears. Whatever reaction your child has to school, by the time winter comes, boredom usually has settled in as well. How can we give our children a boost and encourage them in their academic pursuits?

Evaluating your Present Situation

If your child is struggling in school, ask yourself, "Has my child just made a big transition in school this year?" Maybe your child just began going to school all day instead of just half days.

Also, children may still be anxious about doing "real" work and may continue to worry about their teacher being too strict or about their not being able to keep up with the class. Maybe your child is in a new school this year and is still trying to make friends. Riding the school bus may still be traumatic. I remember one Arp first grader who cried and complained every morning before getting on the school bus all the way up to Christmas! If you want to help your young child, remember that a dose of compassion will go a long way.

The transition from elementary to middle or junior high school can also be a scary time for both parent and child. With this transition comes more freedom. For the kids this can be exhilarating; for the parents, frightening! Maybe your child moved into a larger school with more kids. Also, kids vary greatly in size and development. An eleven-year-old girl can look sixteen while your son the same age still looks like a little boy.

We need to be as understanding as possible. "Don't trivialize their concerns with remarks like, 'Oh, you worry too much,'" says Dr. Balter, psychology professor at New York University and author of *Who's in Control?* "Encourage them to talk to you about their fears. And when offering advice, don't be intrusive."[1] That is, offer your wisdom as suggestion only, not as demand.

If this is a year of transitions in your family, you might take a Transition Checkup.

Taking a Transition Checkup

List recent transitions and changes in your family. (Maybe your child's best friend just moved away, or your child just got glasses, discovered a learning disability, started a new after-school program, or began a new sport activity.)

Transitions and changes I observe are

1.
2.

89

3.

4.

Transitions can bring out your encouragement and helpfulness in letting your child know your interest in how she feels. We can even create positive transition traditions like celebrating the first day of winter with a Just-Me-and-Mom Time.

Just-Me-and-Mom Time for First Day of Winter

To let your child know you understand, plan a special Just-Me-and-Mom Time for the first day of winter. You may even be starting a new winter tradition! Be ready to listen to all the details of what is going on at school. If your child is normally quiet, have your own list of questions ready.

On the first day of winter arrange to pick up your child after school and stop off for a cup of hot chocolate or your child's favorite snack. If you have a turtle who is not talkative, use some of the following open-ended statements:

- What I like most about school this year is . . .
- What I like least about school this year is . . .
- My favorite class . . .
- My least favorite class . . .
- My best friend . . .
- My favorite school lunch . . .
- My most difficult assignment . . .
- My goal for the year is . . .

Making School Mornings Manageable

Getting our children off to school each morning is sometimes just as traumatic as school itself. You may not experience a

90

shower dilemma in your house, but most families suffer some form of getting-kids-off-to-school trauma.

One friend, who is a single mom, came up with her own solution. The night before an extra hectic day, she let her young children sleep in their favorite sweats, and presto! The next morning they were already dressed and ready for school. Whatever our situations, most of us can use some morning simplifiers. Consider the following possible helps:

Prepackaging School Clothes

The next time you do laundry, recruit your child to help. As you are folding the clothes, let your child put several school outfits together—complete with socks, underwear, ribbons, belts, jeans, and whatever else makes up a complete outfit. Then package each outfit or hang the outfits together on coat hangers, and place them in your child's closet. On busy mornings, instead of calling, "Mom, what can I wear?" your child can make a personal selection in record time. And just think—it may match!

Warning: Do not let a young child play with plastic bags. An alternative to plastic bags is to package outfits in the mesh bags that are designed to go in washing machines. You can see through them, and also they can be recycled over and over. One mom in MOM's Support Group suggested using the mesh bags onions and potatoes come in. Of course, you will need to wash the bags before you put clothes in them.

Choosing a Breakfast Helper

Let the children take turns being the official breakfast helper. The job description for the breakfast helper is to set the table the night before. If it is a cereal morning, your child can put the cereal boxes on the table. It is the breakfast helper's job to get up ten minutes early to be available to help Mom with any last minute duties.

Having a Morning Devotion Time

Make family devotions a natural part of your morning routine. We found that if we read just one Bible verse and prayed together, our days went much, much better. The key is to

- Keep it simple. We had our devotion time as part of our breakfast. It rarely lasted over five minutes. This made it practical enough that we actually did it!

92

- Keep it relevant. If a child has a test that day, he'll be willing to have you join him in praying for him to do his best.
- Use simple helps and change them from time to time. We used successfully a devotional guide to Scripture reading, *The Living Light,* (Tyndale, Wheaton, IL) and also a loaf of Bible verses (Warner Press, Anderson, IN). Each day you choose one verse from the small "loaf" of bread, read the verse, and discuss it. We also have used calendars with a verse a day. Or you could make your own jar of Bible verses. Let each child write out several favorite verses, fold each verse separately, and put the slips in a jar. Take turns drawing a verse to read at breakfast.

These suggestions assume that you are eating breakfast together as a family. If you aren't, why not begin? Keep it simple. You'll benefit from starting the day together. Praying together and sharing your thoughts and concerns will help you build family unity.

Do you need some simple breakfast suggestions? Consider the following:

Making Breakfast Quickies

Toast toppers:

Crisp, hot toast was a favorite at our house. Dress toast up with these toast toppers:

- Orange Sugar—Blend 1 tablespoon soft butter and 3 tablespoons sifted powdered sugar. Stir in 1 teaspoon grated orange rind and 1 teaspoon orange juice. Spread on unbuttered toast.
- Cranberry—Spread hot toast with cranberry jelly. Sprinkle with powdered sugar.

- Cinnamon Mix—Combine 1 teaspoon cinnamon and 2 tablespoons sugar. Sprinkle on hot buttered toast. Cut the toast in strips.
- Raisin Peanut Butter—Mix ½ cup crunchy peanut butter, 2 tablespoons chopped seedless raisins and 2 tablespoons orange juice. Spread on hot toast.

Breakfast Fruit Treats:

- A Taste of Hawaii—strawberries and pineapple chunks
- Tropical Morning—sliced bananas in orange juice
- Polka-Dot Day Brightener—raisins sprinkled on applesauce
- Cool Combo—strawberries and seedless grapes

Tricks and Treats with Cereals:

- Serve strawberries over a big bowl of Wheaties.
- Make a raisin face in a bowl of instant oatmeal or Cream of Wheat.
- Top a bowl of Cheerios with half a peach. Add raisin eyes, a maraschino cherry nose, and an apple slice mouth.

How to Get Your Child to Study

Part of beating the winter blues is coping with homework hassles. If you have a secret formula for motivating kids to study, let me know. We'll franchise it and make a fortune! Joel was the most laid back and seemingly unmotivated Arp. I remember Joel's seventeenth birthday. It was the beginning of his senior year in high school, and we were having our birthday celebration meal at a really nice restaurant. Feeling like the successful parent, I asked him, "Joel, what did I do over the years that motivated you the most?" His answer let me know I still had a way to go in winning the motivate-your-kid award. His answer was one word, two syllables: "Nothing!"

Over the years parents have tried "everything" to get their

children to perform up to their abilities in school. They have begged, rewarded, ignored, fought, schemed, punished, and cried.

Unfortunately, there are no quick formulas for turning under-achievers into Einsteins or lazy students into motivated ones. But I do know that our attitude as parents can help or hurt our child's educational progress.

First Check Your Own Attitudes!

"We can change no other person by direct action; we can only change ourselves. When we change, others tend to change in response to us." We use these statements in our Marriage Alive Workshop to help mates relate to each other, but they also apply to our children.

Sometimes, we slip into negative thinking about our children and their school situations, and our negative attitude can hinder their progress. Let's check out our own attitudes, and see if there are some ways we need to change.

Making an Attitude Check!

Ask yourself two questions and reflect on your answers:

1. Are you trying to make your daughter into all you never were in school? You were shy, so you want her to be outgoing. You were an average student, so you want her to make all A's. Does your heart sink when you don't see her name on the honor roll list?

2. Do you expect your child to fail in the areas you didn't do well in? One mom in our MOM's Support Group asked for prayer for her daughter who was getting ready to take the SAT. "I just know she won't do well. I never could do well on standardized tests, and I know she's just like I am." What do you think her attitude commu-

nicated to her daughter? Let's just say it wasn't a confidence builder!

I Love You, Period

We need to make sure our children know that our love and acceptance of them is not based on their performance in school or elsewhere. Sure, we expect the best and hold them accountable for their actions, but we need to talk about reasonable expectations. If C is average, lots of kids out there are going to do their best and still get C's.

Let go of that preconceived notion you had when your child was two and could already recite her ABC's. There are very few children in school today whose parents didn't, at some age, label them gifted. Children learn so quickly in preschools and mother's day out programs. If you decided back then that your child was a genius and have stubbornly held onto that belief, it may be time to let go and take a realistic look at your child.

Some children don't excel in school because they are afraid of failure. School guidance director Gary Sinclair says, "Many sincere Christian parents have unknowingly created a 'No-mistakes-here' atmosphere in their homes because they never talk about their own faults and shortcomings. Children especially need to know that they can feel free to fail and will not be condemned for it!"[2]

You need to assess your child's present school status. Find out from the school how your child compares with other children of the same age and grade. Is your child weak in areas like reading comprehension and math? Are there physical problems like poor eye sight, attention deficit syndrome, or hearing problems?

Do whatever you can to cultivate a healthy academic environment. Our children come with very different temperamental traits and abilities. But however different our children are, they all need some structure and discipline to succeed in school.

As parents, we can do some things to help them develop basic study skills. Consider the following activities:

Creating a Homework Center

Most parents provide a desk or place to study in their children's rooms. Yet most children study somewhere else! Why? If your kids are like most kids, they want to be near the hub of activity, and their rooms just don't qualify. One mom found a great solution. She created a homework center right around the kitchen table. A file box held school supplies that were readily available and also could be put away quickly when her homework center became the evening dinner table. She also took time each afternoon to be on call at the homework center to answer questions and encourage her two children.

Creating a Homework Helper Box

Purchase a cardboard storage box. Let your children decorate the outside of the box with stickers and stencils. Put needed school supplies in the box. You might include

- Paper
- Pencils
- Pencil sharpener
- Glue sticks
- Felt-tip pens
- Rulers
- Scissors
- Theme folders

- Dictionary
- Thesaurus
- Markers

A Trip to an Office Supply Store

I don't know what it is about our family, but we have always loved office supply stores. So don't miss out on a fun field trip with your child. Go to an office supply store, and purchase your supplies for your Homework Helper Box. You can even get the box there! Remember to make a list of what you need *before* you go to the store.

Record-a-Homework

To keep an accurate record of homework assignments and accomplishments, record both. Use a portable cassette recorder and let each child have a tape and make daily recordings. For double entry, write assignments and completions in a homework notebook as well.

Starting the At-Least-Fifteen-Minutes-a-Day Tradition

How can you teach a child to study who daily says, "I don't have any homework!" Start the fifteen-minutes-a-day study tradition. If your child has no homework, provide a fifteen-minute reading assignment or activity to help him develop the habit of studying and broaden his knowledge. For an occasional treat, provide him with an educational video to watch.

Creating a Mom's School for Younger Children

A younger child who doesn't have any homework may feel left out. Look at the child's papers and give some homework from Mom. You could assign a page to color or writing a page of ABC's or numbers. Reward the effort with a sticker or treat.

For the child who complains about bedtime being too early, let her have extra time if she reads in bed.

Surviving Parent-Teacher Conferences

If you've ever felt nervous and apprehensive about a conference with your child's teacher, you're not alone! There is something intimidating about going into a classroom. It can bring back memories of when you were the child and the teacher was the grown-up. Besides, it's not fun to enter a situation knowing that somebody might have something less than flattering to say about your child.

Hopefully, this is not the first time you are meeting your child's teacher. We always tried to take advantage of School and/ or PTA open houses to visit the school and meet the teachers in an informal setting. My goal on those occasions was to let my presence show our children's teachers that I cared for my child and that education was important in our family.

When you actually do have a parent-teacher conference, you can do several things to handle the conference in a positive way:

99

- Present a united front. The ideal situation is for Mom and Dad to go together. While this is not always an option, it is the ideal.
- Remember that the meeting is to help your child, and keep a positive attitude.
- Make a list of things you want to ask or talk about and arrange your list so that the most important items are at the top. Take the list with you and refer to it during the conference.
- Be on time.
- Jot down any teacher suggestions. Don't be afraid to ask questions.
- Listen carefully to what the teacher says. One way to make sure you do listen is to paraphrase what the teacher says to you. This may help prevent misunderstandings.

You may want to ask your child's teacher general questions:

- Where is my child's desk?
- What is the grading scale?
- Will you give standardized tests? When are they given?
- What is the homework policy?
- How does my child relate to others in the class?

You may want to share some special things with your child's teacher:

- Special situations at home
- Medical problems
- Personal achievements of your child beyond academics
- How your child is motivated by praise, for instance, rather than reprimand

Volunteers Needed

One of the most beneficial things I discovered in relating to my children's teachers was to volunteer to help in some way. When the boys were young, I helped in the classroom one morning a week. Sometimes I worked with the slow readers or other students who needed individual help. The whole time I could observe my child and see firsthand how he related to his teacher and to the rest of the class. As the boys became older and were in middle school and high school, I stayed involved, but from a distance. My work was still quite educational! I might help in the library or with the PTA concession booth, or I might facilitate a Mom's and Dad's Support Group. (For information on how to start a Mom's and Dad's Support Group see the information page in the back of this book.)

Being involved in our children's school has many benefits for us, for the teachers, and also for our children. I'll never forget the day I won the parent-to-the-rescue award from Jonathan. He was in the second grade and had the dreaded Mrs. Galpin who was an excellent teacher but unrelentingly strict with the students. We had actually requested Mrs. Galpin. I was in the classroom that morning helping with a reading group when I observed a look of distress on Jonathan's face. I could see his dilemma. A container of yogurt had spilled inside his desk. He was too scared to tell Mrs. Galpin, and I could just imagine what spilled yogurt would smell like after a few days of incubation.

As the children were dismissed for recess, I simply walked over to the sink, took several paper towels, and cleaned up the mess. There was a raised eyebrow but no comment from Mrs. Galpin, and a great look from Jonathan. His look said, "Mom, you are the greatest, and I'm so relieved I'm going to live!" Not only did I save some sanity that day; from Jonathan's perspective I saved his life!

Now it's your turn. Take the risk; get involved in creating schooltime sanity. Whether it's harnessing homework hassles, prepackaging school clothes, serving a surprise breakfast, or cleaning up yogurt, you too may win the parent-to-the-rescue award!

7

Sports: Whose Game Is It?

The morning air was crisp and cool. The day seemed perfect for what Susan and her family spent most Saturday mornings doing—watching their children play soccer. The game began, and the antics of the parents on the sidelines were as intense as the action on the field.

Actually, on this particular day, the sideline action was far more intense than the game. The children were trying to have a good time; the parents were trying to win.

Other days the comments yelled at the kids from the sidelines were overwhelmingly positive: "Great kick, Billy!" "Good running, Spencer!" "Don't let that bother you, Brett! You did great!"

But this morning, one of the coaches was screaming. There's a distinct difference in tone between yelling and screaming when it comes to sideline voices, and this was screaming. His players could do nothing to please him. The real clincher was that the coach's own son was the primary target of his anger: "What are you doing out there, Peter?" "Wake up, Peter!" "How could you let that ball get past you?" "Just give it to them. Let them have the whole game! You might as well have stayed home!"

Finally, Susan could stand it no longer. She stepped up behind Peter's dad and gently tapped him on the shoulder.

"My voice was trembling, both from anger and fear," she told me, "but I told him to give those kids a break and try some positive coaching." She added a point that he had obviously forgotten. "It's only a game. The kids are supposed to be out here to have a good time."

If you think this is a horror story, read on. The children in this soccer game were first graders! Six year olds should not have to face that kind of pressure!

Very few topics elicit as much emotion as sports and your child. We live in a sports-oriented society, and unless you are a hermit or live in a monastery, sports will probably affect you in one way or another this winter. What can we do as parents to ensure that sports will be a positive, instead of a negative, influence in our children's lives?

Sports Motivation Checkup

First you need to look at why you want your child to participate in sports. Check the following statements that apply to you:

____ "I want my child to be in sports for the exercise."
____ "All my child's friends are playing, and I don't want my child to feel left out."
____ "I want my child to learn to be part of a team and learn good sportsmanship and competition."
____ "I think my child will enjoy sports, and I know I will enjoy helping!"

Obviously the last reason is the most valid and should always be the primary factor.

There are also other, more subtle reasons. These are not necessarily bad reasons, but you need to recognize them if they do exist. It will help you evaluate what to do if things don't work out the way you hoped.

Check the following statements that apply to you:

____ "I secretly want to be the parent of a superstar."

____ "I want to get my child out of my hair for a while each week."

____ "Our family needs something to focus on, and sports seems like a good choice."

____ "Our older child is already an athlete."

____ "I love to win and compete, so I know my child will."

If most of your reasons for wanting your child to participate are in the second set of statements, make sure that your child really wants to play the sport. Sports are definitely all-American but not a utopia for everyone.

Consider one family we know. Their two boys, Craig and Nick, played soccer. Nick took to soccer the way a duck takes to water. He loved the physical part of the game, and competition could have been his middle name. Craig, on the other hand, just didn't like contact sports and tolerated soccer instead of enjoying it. *I'm in this family,* he thought, *so guess I have to play soccer.*

Craig was one of the fortunate kids. His parents, understanding his sensitive nature and lack of interest in soccer, allowed him to quit and begin piano lessons. What happened? We were with his family recently, and Craig proudly entertained us with his music. He didn't like playing soccer, but he just may be the next Mozart! And just because Craig didn't enjoy soccer, his parents didn't rule out sports. Last summer they actually hired our son Jonathan to give both Craig and Nick tennis lessons.

Tennis is an individual sport that both boys enjoy. Now the whole family plays tennis.

Our friends and their two sons modeled some great principles that can help other families.

- They exposed their kids to several different sports.
- They supported their children's individual interests.
- They provided help in skill development.
- They let the sport be the child's sport.

Let's examine these four principles a little more closely.

Exposing Your Child to Sports

Neither Dave nor I comes from a sport-oriented family. Neither did we plan to have three sports-loving sons, but I still remember the day we realized if we were going to spend time together as a family, we would have to give some time to sports.

For unathletic me this was quite a revelation! Since both Dave and I like to participate, instead of just being a spectators, it was time to do a little planning and goal setting.

We knew that down the road organized sports would probably be a given with our boys, but what could we do at the early stage to capitalize on our boys' keen interest in sports and build our family at the same time? We decided to choose a couple of sports that we could learn and participate in together.

In our imaginations, we fast-forwarded to the future. Wouldn't it be great if there were a couple of things—like sports—that we could begin to do now as a family, sports that our kids would still enjoy doing with us as teenagers and as adults!

We had already heard the predictions of the turbulent teenage years. Perhaps we could do a little preventative work that would actually smooth out some of the rough spots in those years. For instance, we knew that if we started a sport in our thirties and our boys started the same sport in childhood, by the teenage years, they would be more proficient at that sport than we were. Now I can tell you from experience that it does help parent-teen relationships if in some activities the teen outperforms the parent!

So at the Arp house, we decided to pick a winter sport and a summer sport to learn together. Since we lived in Austria, it was natural for us to choose snow skiing for winter. We could drive an hour from our home, ski as long as our boys lasted, have our hot chocolate and sandwiches in the car, and drive home for about ten dollars. In this sport our boys outperformed their mom from the very beginning.

For a summer sport we picked tennis. I had an edge here, but notice I'm writing in past tense. Note, too, that we played tennis as a family. We didn't just sign our kids up for lessons and drop them off and pick them up. It took buckets of balls and pails of patience, but we persevered. And in the end our efforts paid rich dividends. We still enjoy our two family sports. We can go for long periods of time without skiing—I'm talking years—and still pick it up and enjoy being together.

Our family sports naturally led into competitive sports. All three boys raced competitively in snow skiing, and one played tournament tennis through high school. All three played competitive soccer at one time or another. The Arps were even known to play tag football together. We divided up into teams of two and three. The team with three got Mom and was spotted one touchdown!

Maybe you are thinking, *That's great for you, but I'm just not athletic.* That really doesn't have very much to do with it. I'm definitely not the athletic type, but we can all enjoy sports for fun. Stop right now and think about different sports that you could do with your family. Right now in the empty nest, Dave and I walk together several times a week. (We find it quite sporting!) Your sport doesn't have to be elaborate or expensive. We used to go to a fitness park with our boys and do the fitness course as a family. Of course, the boys laughed at me when I tried to do the chin-ups.

Sports Possibilities for My Family

List different sports your family might want to learn to do to-gether:

1.
2.
3.
4.

After doing some initial research, you may want to call a family meeting to discuss your own family game plan and choose a winter sports activity to share.

A Family Sports Caucus

List as many different sports as you can think of. Use two categories: team sports and individual sports. Talk about which ones the family might be interested in pursuing.

Team Sports (softball, soccer, football, basketball, volley-ball, hockey; for preschoolers and toddlers, you might add tag, keep-away, and hide-and-seek):

1.
2.
3.
4.
5.
6.

Individual Sports (tennis, wrestling, gymnastics, track, swimming, golf, bowling, table tennis, bicycling, ice skating, archery):

1.
2.
3.
4.
5.

Sports we want to try are

1.
2.
3.
4.

Trying sports as a family provides good initial exposure. It gives your child a chance to try activities without being embarrassed by peers. It can also lead to back-yard athletics with friends. For us one thing led to another and eventually to competitive sports.

Supporting Your Child's Interest in Sports

As you begin to explore sports together as a family, you will probably notice that your child is drawn to one or two specific sports. Now is the time for giving support to your child.

If your child is interested in playing on a team, help your child find a team or league he or she can join. This may take some effort on your part. Talk to the coaches. Try to find out their coaching style. How important is winning to the coach? Does your child already know other children on the team? Is the league recreational or highly competitive? Will traveling be involved? What expenses will you incur?

Many, if not most, of the coaches your children will encounter will be wonderful, kind, loving human beings who care deeply for the emotional and psychological well-being of your child. Cherish them, assist them, and encourage your child to make the best of the experience. Organized sports can add a new dimension to your children's lives.

Mistakes Parents Make

In our desire to help our children excel in sports, we may err in several ways.

First, we may push our children too soon. Three-year-old Billy strutted onto the tennis court. His junior size racket was almost as big as he was. It was time for his private tennis lesson. The intense expression on his mother's face reminded me of other mothers I've read about like Mrs. Everett, Mrs. Connors, and Mrs. Chang. Could Billy be a tennis star in the twenty-first century? I could tell this mom certainly hoped so!

In *Sports and Your Child*, Cliff Schimmels and J. R. Bishop put it this way: "Sports, particularly for children, should be fun. The child should develop his own interest. There are far more dangers in starting a child too early than in starting one too late. Use your child's interest as a deciding factor on when to start."[1]

Next, we push our children to pursue our own interests. The dad who was the big football star—or wishes he had been—insists that his son will go out for football. On the other hand, friends of ours who both played professional tennis have a son who plays soccer and baseball. He plays tennis as well, but it's out of his own interest. We watched him playing his very first tournament at age ten, and we appreciated his parents refusal to apply pressure.

Sometimes, too, we do not allow our children to change their minds. We have a "You-started-it-and-you-have-to-finish-it" mentality—even if our children are in a damaging situation.

If a child doesn't enjoy playing or isn't very good at it and is ridiculed, humiliation and rejection may be the only lessons learned. Don't be afraid to let your child quit.

If your child ends up on a team whose coach has lost sight of the whole purpose of sport—to have a good time, to build self-esteem, to fine-tune developing motor skills—or if a coach is negative with your child, pull the child off the team. If your child isn't enjoying the experience, let him quit without the quitter lecture. You will make him finish plenty of other things. If your

109

child is in a really negative situation, don't let this be one of them, for bad sports experiences can cause major damage.

Think about it. We parents would step in front of a speeding train to protect our children from physical harm. We need to protect our children's emotional well-being too. Do not stand on the sidelines while a volunteer parent who has been labeled "coach" belittles and ridicules your child.

Finally, sometimes we parents forget that it is just a game. Have you seen the poster that says, "Tennis is not a matter of life or death—it's more important than that!" We laugh, but I still remember one of Jonathan's tournaments. It was a tight three-set match. He seemed to have the edge, but in the end he lost. Later he said, "Mom, I started thinking about my opponent. I know the pressure his parents put on him, and I started thinking about what he would have to face when he got home if I beat him. I lost my concentration!"

Please, oh, please, ask yourself, "Whose game is it?" If it is yours, it's time to regroup!

Helping Your Child Develop Skills

What can we parents do to help our children develop skills in their chosen sport or sports? First, realize that some children have more natural athletic ability than others. Some children have better skills than others. The first we can't influence, but we can help our children develop skills. Coaches have many stories of athletes with average ability who made themselves winners by learning skills and techniques. The good news is that skills are learned!

Coaches Bishop and Schimmels say, "If you are interested in your child becoming a winner or developing a winning attitude through athletic participation, one of your major tasks is to make sure that the skills are practiced. Get some instruction on the right technique. After that, it is just a matter of practice, practice, practice, practice, and practice."

Then they add this stern warning:

If you send your child out to play any youth league sport without having provided an opportunity for practicing the basic skills, you should be arrested for child abuse. I have seen that child, standing out in right field in the middle of a ball game, surrounded by watching playmates and friends, and the poor kid has never seen a fly ball, much less caught one. That is criminal. No one should do that to any human being. If you don't have time to go out in the back yard and practice with your child, pay somebody to do it."[2]

And that's not a bad idea. Why not organize a sports clinic right in your own back yard?

Organizing a Skills Clinic

1. Check with your church sports ministry or youth director or with a school or league coach and find kids who have the skills your child needs to develop and who want to earn some money while helping younger children.
2. Set a time and place, like every Monday afternoon right after school in your yard.
3. Call the parents of your child's friends who are also involved in the same sport (or would like to be). Invite their children to participate. Each child pays a fee for each clinic—like two dollars per afternoon.
4. Provide snacks and drinks for the hungry mob.
5. Watch as your child builds confidence and enjoyment in this sports activity!

These clinics actually work. The Arps have held them. In Vienna, our boys organized soccer clinics in our back yard. They had fun, earned some money, and greatly helped and encouraged the younger kids. By the way, one of the former "students" is the lead scorer on the Georgetown University varsity soccer team! (The student obviously passed up his teachers!)

Taking a Lesson with Your Child

Don't overlook the fun of sharing a lesson with your child. I can remember taking tennis lessons with Jarrett. Try it. It may be a fun Just-Me-and-Mom Time, and your own athletic skills may improve as well!

Observing the Experts

Take your child to a professional game of his favorite sport. Children learn by watching the experts. If this is not possible in your local area, watch TV sports with your child.

What Do the Athletes Eat?

As a family, research sports nutrition. What do the star athletes eat before a big game? Do a study of the four types of food, and plan a healthy diet for the next week.

What's Your Condition?

Discuss the importance of conditioning and being in shape. Choose simple exercises, and do them together as a family. If you don't know what to do, ask your child's coach for suggestions.

Building Your Own Soccer Goal or Tennis Backboard

A good way to give your children an edge is to provide equipment that will help them practice. One dad I know is presently building his sons a soccer goal. We built a tennis backboard for Jonathan out of two-by-fours and treated plywood, and we painted it green. It wasn't too expensive and definitely gave him an edge.

Let the Sport Be Your Child's

Remember why you are encouraging your children to participate in sports. The number one reason should be to have a good time. They will also learn to accept both success and failure, and they will learn the rewards of hard work. They will develop motor skills. If the experience is a good one, they will build self-esteem.

All these lessons can be learned more effectively with the backdrop of supportive parents who realize just whose game it really is. To keep the proper attitude and approach toward sports, remember the following:

- Emphasize the fun of actually playing the sport.
- Win or lose, treat your child the same.
- Never make gifts and rewards contingent upon winning or losing.
- Help your children make honest evaluations of their ability.[3]
- Actually participate in the sport with your child if possible.

Personally Applied

On the first day in late winter that the weather cooperated, Jonathan was trying out for the school tennis team. He and I were getting a head start on spring training. As we walked onto the court, I thought it only fair to warn him: "Jonathan, I just want you to know this year I'm giving you no breaks. I'm going to play my best tennis and let the chips fall where they may. I want to remind you, whenever we lose, that character is built through failure. You'll improve much more quickly in your game if I force you to play your best."

That being said, I proceeded to hit the balls as hard as I could. Competition was alive and well that day. I did get a couple of games in one set, but Jonathan beat me decisively. As a matter of fact, I've never won a set from him since—and I've had many, many opportunities to build character!

Give your children the support and help they need in their own choices, and you will see athletics build character for your whole family. This is one winter endeavor in which you can all win!

8

Snow Days, Sick Days, and We've-Got-Nothing-to-Do Days

"The first snow day is a party!" So said my friend, Sherri. "It's the one time each year," she added, "that I qualify for the super-mom award."

"You've got to be kidding." I responded, but Sherri wasn't kidding at all! It's the one day of the year she is prepared for, and you can be too!

Packing a Snow Party

It's time to pack your snow boxes! When it snows, you'll be ready. Who cares if there's no school? So what if you can't get your car out of your driveway? The snow box will be ready, and the fun can begin.

The wonders of a snow box are the simple pleasures it holds. You fill your snow box with everything you need for a snow party. The basics for Sherri's snow party are

- 6 cans of Beanie Weenies™
- 1 canister of hot chocolate mix
- 1 bag of marshmallows
- 2 cans of chili beans
- 1 package of mild chili seasoning mix
- 4 cans of tomato sauce
- 1 box of Rice Krispies™
- 1 small jar of peanut butter
- 1 small bottle of corn syrup
- 1 Ziploc™ bag (or margarine tub) with at least 1 cup of sugar in it
- 1 pair of gloves per child and adult
- 1 hat per child and adult
- 1 pair of snow boots or plastic shoe covers per child and adult
- 1 craft kit

The only things you need for a great snow day that can't be put in the snow box are one pound of ground beef or turkey and a festive mood. (The ground meat should be frozen and hidden way back in the back of the freezer so that no one will find it.) Put it under the turkey slices you froze after Thanksgiving, the ones you were going to use in a casserole some day.

The Beanie Weenies™ are for lunch. Feel free to substitute your own favorite canned lunch. The requirements are that it be quick, easy, storable, and cheap enough to share with snow party friends.

The craft kit isn't complicated. Consider the following:

- A bag of different colors of yarn and ribbon that can be made into friendship bracelets
- A bag of ribbons for making hair bows
- An air-dry pottery clay kit
- Ingredients to make play dough (see pages 126–127 for recipe)

The remaining food items are for the staples of a snow party and include dinner with the menu of chili, hot chocolate with marshmallows, and quick peanut butter krispies. The recipe is simple:

Peanut Butter Krispies

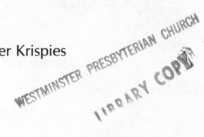

½ cup sugar
½ cup light corn syrup
2 cups Rice Krispies
1 cup peanut butter

In a medium glass bowl, stir the sugar and corn syrup. Microwave on high for 3 minutes or until the mixture comes to a full boil. Stir in the cereal and peanut butter. Drop teaspoonfuls of the mixture onto waxed paper.

You can also hide a roll of slice-and-bake chocolate chip cookies in the freezer with the ground meat.

Even if your children have gloves and hats, buy extra sets. The ones they wear every day are sure to be left at school the day before it snows.

The festive mood is easier to acquire because your snow box is ready. Put towels down from the door to the kitchen, empty the dryer, call the neighborhood kids to come over with an extra set of clothes, bundle everyone up for their five minutes of playing outside, and let the party begin! Be sure to join in the fun—even if you come inside after only two minutes. When the whole gang comes inside, make them change clothes in the laundry room, and put everything in the dryer. That way it's all ready for the next outside play, usually about forty-five minutes after they've come in from the first one. (If the clothes are dirty, other moms may not want them to go into the dryer. It sets dirt in the fibers.) Have extra clothes for "mad days."

With your snow party box all assembled, you can face the winter knowing that for at least one day you are going to be very popular! So let it snow—you will be ready![1]

I don't know what it was about snow and cooking, but our three children loved to help Mom cook on those days. You might recruit some help in preparing breakfast. Apple drop biscuits are a special treat and easy to make.

Making Apple Drop Biscuits

Ingredients:

2 cups Bisquick
2 tablespoons sugar
1/2 teaspoon cinnamon
1/4 teaspoon nutmeg
1 small apple, peeled
1/2 cup apple juice

Directions: Preheat the oven to 450 degrees. Shred the apple. Combine Bisquick, sugar, cinnamon, and nutmeg. Pour the apple juice into a bowl; add the Bisquick mixture and shredded apples. Stir with a wooden spoon until wet. The batter should be lumpy, so don't stir it too much.

Grease a cookie sheet. Drop the mixture by tablespoons onto the cookie sheet. Bake 10 to 12 minutes.

These are especially good with honey butter.

Like the snow box, other cooking supplies can be kept on hand, ready for any possibility. It's easy to make a Snowman Cake for a fun impromptu winter party.

Making a Snowman Cake

Grease and flour two round layer pans, one 8 by 1½ inches and one 9 by 1½ inches. Prepare any flavor cake mixes as directed on the package, divide the batter between the two pans, and bake.

On a foil-covered cardboard, place the 8-inch layer for the head of the snowman and the 9-inch layer for the body. Using a white frosting mix, frost the layers, joining them together. Sprinkle with flaked coconut.

Use semisweet chocolate pieces for buttons; gumdrops for eyes, eyebrows, and the nose; red shoestring licorice for the mouth; and red rope licorice for the muffler. Place a large chocolate wafer cookie on each side of head for earmuffs.

On days you wish it would snow, make your own paper snowflakes.

Making a Snowflake

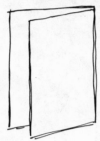

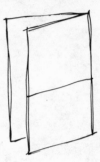

1. Fold a square of paper in half.

2. Mark the center of folded square as shown.

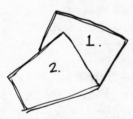

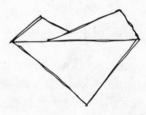

3. Fold it again like this. Mark the parts 1 and 2.

4. Fold 1 over 2 and then turn the paper over.

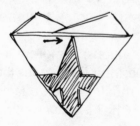

5. Draw a design up to arrow and cut it out without unfolding.

6. The cut-out design is your paper snowflake. Draw different designs, and you will have a collection of paper snowflakes.

Sick Days

Sick days may follow snow days—especially if the children slipped out into the snow without warm clothes or stayed out too long or traded germs with a friend. Whatever the cause, most families have a few sick days sprinkled into the winter months. These days are not fun, but are easier to deal with if you are prepared. Here are some suggestions that will help you survive sick days at your house.

A Sick Day Drawer or Shelf

In a special drawer or on a shelf, compile supplies for sick days. Books, quiet games, simple craft kits, and a special video or audio tape are appreciated by a child who is under the weather and has to stay at home.

Making a Patient Chart

Pamper your sick child by making his very own health chart on a clipboard. Record temperature and medicine—what was taken and when. You can also record food eaten and liquids drunk. Have a special page where visitors can sign in and out.

The "Sick" Bell

Every child (of any age) loves to have a bell by the bed to call the slaves to come when needed. (I even like this one!) Let family members take turns being on call.

Make a Sick Companion

Does your young child hate being in bed my herself? Make her a companion. Cover a small pillow with an old pillow case, a white towel, or a cloth, and draw a face. Use yarn for hair and buttons for eyes. Now your child has a "companion" to hug and talk to when she is bored.

Tape-a-Book

In your free time (before child gets sick if possible), record books on cassettes. For younger children add a "beep" so they can follow along and turn the pages. This will entertain your sick child for short periods of time and give you a break!

Viewing Family Photo Albums

Let your sick child look through old family photo albums. It will help him remember good times and look forward to fun times in the future.

Making a Lap Desk

Make a lap desk from an empty packing box. Cut a half-circle in the two long sides of the box and leave the ends as they are. Cover the box with contact paper, or let the child draw on the lap desk and color it. The lap desk will fit nicely over your patient as he sits in the bed.

Making a Pencil Box

Make a companion pencil and supply box from a shoe box. Cover it with the same contact paper. Add pencils, crayons, a small note pad, and anything else you want. I don't know why, but all of our boys loved to play with Band-Aids™.

Of course, days home with a sick child will not be your most productive days. So relax, and grab the opportunity to have that special one-to-one time.

We've-Got-Nothing-to-Do Days

With snow days, bad weather days, and sick days, boredom too often comes along. What can you do on those days you hear that broken record: "Mommy, I've got nothing to do"? Here are some boredom busters.

Creating Fun!

Many things that we normally throw away can feed a child's imagination. Add some glue, felt-tip pens, crayons, tempera paint, and tape, and just watch what your child can create. To get you started, here is a list of possible things to save—and suggested items to be made from each:

Creating Through Recycling

Things to Save	Things to Make
Paper rolls	Telescope, megaphone, binoculars
Oatmeal boxes	Rocket ships, drums
Milk cartons	Pull trains and blocks
Shoe boxes	Doll house rooms
Sheets	Tent, sleeping bags
Empty cans, string	Telephone, stilts
Eggs and milk cartons	Castle, caterpillar
Socks, nylons	Sock puppets, old faces
Corks, sponges	Boats
Boxes of all sizes	Cage, doll bed and house, cars, planes, trucks, barn
Paper clips	Necklace and jewelry

Making a Garbage Gobbler

Wash and dry a large bleach bottle. Cut the top almost all the way off, leaving a hinge near the handle. Cut out and glue paper face features and yarn hair onto the bottle. Then keep the room clean by feeding all your garbage to the Gobbler!

Toothpick Sculptures

You need toothpicks and marshmallows.
Use the marshmallows to hold the toothpicks together as you build a sculpture.

Tongue Twisters

Try to say each of these tongue twisters five times in a row as fast as you can.

- A critical cricket critic.
- Tim, the thin twin tinsmith.
- Does this shop stock short socks with spots?
- Tom threw Tim three thumbtacks.
- Slim Sam slid sideways.
- The dude dropped in at the Dewdrop Inn.
- Rubber baby buggy bumpers.
- A black-backed bath brush.

Mixing Colors

What you need: four glasses; water; and yellow, red, and blue food coloring.

Fill three glasses with water and have your child put drops of each color into separate glasses to make blue, yellow, and red water. Now your child can mix the colored water in the other glass to see what other colors they can make. (Yellow and red will make orange; yellow and blue will make green; and blue and red will make violet.)

Kool-Aid Play Dough

Mix well

2½ cups flour
½ cup salt
1 tablespoon Alum
2 packages unsweetened Kool-Aid

Add:

2 cups boiling water
3 teaspoons cooking oil
Knead until smooth. Let the play dough cool.

Making Mobiles

Materials:

Wire coat hanger
String
Cardboard or construction paper
Aluminum foil
Paints and brushes
Crayons

Instructions: Cut pieces of string of random lengths, and tie them to the bottom of a wire coat hanger. Cut out from construction paper or foil different shapes—hearts, birds, animals, and so on. Decorate with paints or crayons.

Tie each shape to a piece of string and hang from your wire mobile. Suspend your mobile from a single string in a spot where air currents will keep the hanger and decorations moving.

Preparing for Winter Holidays

On those boring days when there is "nothing to do" consider getting a jump on winter holidays. Pull out the craft supplies and make Valentines, Christmas Cards, or Christmas and birthday presents. (See pages 162–167 for suggestions of gifts you can make.) Don't forget President's Day, Martin Luther King Day, and St. Patrick's Day.

Creative Fun with Paper

Paper, now so familiar to us, used to be precious and rare. Before 200 B.C. no such product existed. Then the Chinese developed a form of paper made from the bark of the mulberry tree.

Now we have over seven thousand kinds of paper, all basically made from wood pulp, vegetable fibers, rags, or a combination of these. The fibrous material is chemically treated, beaten, mixed with water, and pressed into paper.

Creating Paper Magic

See how many different kinds of paper your children can find in your home. Almost any kind of paper can be used to create your own magic. Look for

- Construction paper
- Typing paper
- Newsprint
- Cardboard
- Crepe paper
- Tissue paper
- Wallpaper samples
- Newspapers
- Catalogs
- Magazines
- Grocery bags
- Gift wrapping
- Wax paper
- Paper towels
- Facial tissues
- Paper napkins

Create your own magic with paper. Paper can do many things, it starts out flat, and you can put life into it by

- Cutting
- Twisting
- Bending
- Curling
- Scoring
- Fringing
- Scratching
- Folding
- Denting
- Pinching

- Tearing
- Wrinkling
- Punching
- Interlacing
- Pasting
- Stapling
- Marking
- Painting
- Papier mâchéing

Hole Punching

One fun activity with paper is hole punching. Let your child punch holes in colored paper. The confetti that falls to the floor or on the table makes great fine motor pincer play for the younger child. Eventually children can collect it and glue it onto paper or use it to decorate the outsides of small plastic containers. When your child gets tired of confetti play, the mess is easy to vacuum up.

Decorate a House

On a large piece of paper (like newsprint) draw a house frame showing the different rooms, and tape it to a door or a wall. Give your children old catalogs, and let them cut or tear out pictures of furniture, lamps, pictures, people, or anything

129

they want to place in the rooms. Let them paste or tape objects within the house (not on the walls)!

Making a Paper Collage

Using old magazines and catalogs, let your child make a collage of things in God's world that are good for you or things he is thankful for. This will help develop cutting, tearing, and pasting skills and will keep your child busy for quite a while. One mom shared recently that her two children did this activity together on paper plates and got along great, which was quite unusual for them.

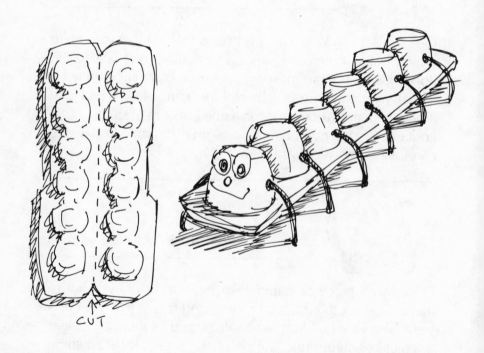

Egg Carton Caterpillar

Materials:

- Empty egg carton
- Pipe cleaners
- Paints and/or crayons
- Construction paper
- Scissors
- Glue

Instructions: Carefully cut the carton in half lengthwise so that the caterpillar has six connected humps when it's turned over. Puncture each hump and insert a pipe cleaner through each segment to form the legs. Cut out paper eyes, nose, and mouth, and glue to the front section of the egg carton. Color the segments with crayons or paint.

Paper Bag Faces

Materials:

- Paper bags
- Cotton puffs
- Yarn

- Crayons
- Scissors
- Glue

Instructions: Depending upon the size of the bag used, these can be either hand puppets or actual children's masks. Cut holes for eyes, nose, and mouth. Use yarn to decorate the head with hair, mustaches, or beards. Glue on cotton puffs for eyebrows or cheeks. Color with felt-tip pens or crayons.

Variation: Use paper plates to make the faces, and tie the plates on the children with yarn or ribbon. Make headbands out of construction paper and decorate them with glitter or color designs. Tie them on with string.

Making a Crawling Alligator

Cut wedges from a tissue box.

Cover the shapes with green paper. Glue the larger ends of the wedges together.

To make the eyes, glue cotton balls on the shorter wedge; use dark paper for the pupils. Glue paper for the mouth and nose, or draw them on with marker or crayon.

Thread a straw or a pipe cleaner through a spool of thread for a wheel and axle. Poke holes in the larger wedge to place the axle on the inside.

Recycling Large Boxes

Save large boxes for your child to make his or her own fort, house, or slide. One mom shared how her daughter created a house, drew in windows with curtains and a mailbox, and used magazine pictures to decorate with flowers.

Fun You Can Eat

Muffin Pizzas

What you need:

English muffins
Tomato sauce or pizza sauce
Mozzarella cheese

Spread the sauce on the muffin, and put on the cheese and any other ingredients you want.

Bake at 450 degrees Fahrenheit for 10 minutes.

Purple Cows

What you need:

1 cup of grape juice
1 scoop ice cream
½ cup milk

Blend juice, milk, and ice cream in a blender.

Chocolate Peanut Butter Sticks

What you need:

8 ounces semi-sweet chocolate chips
6 tablespoons peanut butter
1 teaspoon vanilla
1 cup wheat germ

Melt chocolate chips, and blend with peanut butter and vanilla. Stir in the cup of wheat germ. Press the mixture into a greased 8-inch square pan, and chill until firm. Cut into bars.

Outside Fun

Sometimes even if it's cold outside, we moms need to get the children, as well as ourselves, out of the house. I love one idea that a mother in MOM's Support Group shared with our group.

The Mega Play Pen!

"One day I was desperate for some help. My two- and three-year-old boys were full of energy, and I wasn't. The local park I drove to was muddy, and I wasn't in the right frame of mind for the mess. But there was a tennis court there. As I entered the court with my two boys and the tall fence towered over me, I received a great revelation from God! 'This is a giant play pen!'

"I closed the gate door behind me. There was no mud, I could sit down on the court and not get wet, and someone had sovereignly left two tennis balls on the courts. The boys had thirty minutes of running, throwing the balls over the net, and working off some of their endless energy while I regained some of mine! Next time I'm taking balls, lunch, blankets, and a book!"

Making Bubbles

Combine

    2 cups liquid detergent   3/4 cup corn syrup
    6 cups water

Dip the large end of a kitchen funnel into the bubble mixture, and blow through the small end. You can also make a circle out of a small coat hanger. Dip and blow. The large commercial wands you can buy are fun too. This is a fun activity for the whole family; even the adult "kids" enjoy it! It is less messy if you do it outside!

Nature Scavenger Hunt

Preparation time for mom may take up to ten minutes, but the fun for the kids will usually last at least an hour! Make a list of objects for your children to find in your yard or play ground. (It is important that you give them well-defined boundaries safe for their ages.)

For small children who do not yet recognize words, use crayons and draw the objects for the scavenger hunt. Give each child a list or page with pictures and a bag. Burlap bags with shoulder straps work great and make this activity a real hunting adventure. One mom in a MOM's Support Group suggested the following list of items popular with her six- and eight-year-olds:

- Rocks (find different colors, like a white rock or a brown rock)
- Something fuzzy
- Twig with no leaf
- Twig with a leaf
- Leaves (You can specify colors.)
- Pinecone
- Pine needle
- Dead weed
- Green weed
- Dead bug (For the daring!)

- Moss
- Use your imagination for other possibilities!

After the hunt is over, end the adventure with a snack, and let each child proudly display all the found treasures. You decide what to do with the dead bug!

Keep Them Guessing

One last activity that is guaranteed to bring smiles and laughter and to prevent boredom is to serve surprise sherbet sandwiches. Here's how to pull it off:

Surprise Sherbet Sandwiches

Directions:

Two hours before serving, spoon orange or lime or rainbow sherbet into a six-ounce orange juice can. Cover the top with aluminum foil, and freeze the sherbet for two hours. Remove the foil and the other end of the can. Push out the sherbet and cut it into eight ½-inch slices. Put each slice on the back side of a round butter cookie. Top with another cookie.

Serve surprise sherbet sandwiches on the most boring day you can find. Preferably, it should be a day when the kids have moped around the house, are lazy bums, and finally ate breakfast at 11:00 A.M. An hour after their late breakfast, when they are outside playing, sternly go to the door and call them in for lunch. You will probably hear complaints: "I'm not hungry." "We just ate breakfast." "I don't want anything to eat!"

Respond with, "Well, that's just too bad. It's lunch time, and I've made your sandwiches. You have to come in and eat two sandwiches each before you can play any more!"

As the children grudgingly come to the table, serve sherbet sandwiches and watch the amazed smiles and laughter break out on their faces. You'll find that once again you have chased away boredom and one more winter day has been transformed into fun memories. Try it and prove me right. You can be a winter star at your house!

Part Four

Surviving the Winter Holidaze

9

Thanksgiving

Did you ever consider that Thanksgiving is a uniquely American holiday? We didn't until we lived in Austria. Jarrett and Joel were both in a British school. Imagine their protests when they had to go to school on Thanksgiving Day!

Including our British friends in our Thanksgiving celebrations seemed appropriate until we did it. Suffice it to say the British have a completely different perspective about Thanksgiving. We talked of the Pilgrims who came to America seeking religious freedom and a chance to have a new start. Our British friends talked about rebellion! It all depends on perspective.

Actually, Thanksgiving should be a universal Christian holiday. Throughout the Scriptures, we are admonished to remember what God has done for us and to be thankful. In 1 Samuel 12:24 we read, "Only fear the LORD, and serve Him in truth with all your heart; for consider what great things He has done for you."

How can we help our families express their gratitude to God for all the great things He has done for us? While we don't want to limit our Thanksgiving experience, we can take some cues from the Pilgrims and that first Thanksgiving so many years ago.

Thanksgiving—A Thankful Time

The Pilgrims publicly said thank you to God for the harvest and for their safety. Here are some practical ways we can express our thanks.

"I'm Thankful for . . ."

Together as a family, make a thankful list. Take turns adding to the list. Start with the youngest family member and work up to the oldest. See how many things you can think of. Post your list on the refrigerator, the bulletin board, or wherever your communication center is. Date and save the list as a record of some of the things the Lord has done in your family.

Writing a Thanksgiving Prayer

Have someone in your family write out a special prayer to share at your Thanksgiving dinner.

Answered Prayer Bowl

During the year as you and your children observe ways God answers prayers, write each answer on a piece of paper, fold it, and put it in a special bowl. You may want to keep this bowl in the dining room or somewhere you will see it often. Then as a Thanksgiving tradition, take turns reading the answered prayers during your Thanksgiving dinner.

Thanksgiving—A Peacemaking Time

For the Pilgrims, Thanksgiving was a time of peacemaking. Cranberries—one of our traditional Thanksgiving foods—symbolized peace among early Indian tribes. The story goes that the Indians presented the Pilgrims with gifts of cranberries as a sign of friendship and peace.

String Cranberries

With a blunt needle and course thread, string cranberries. Put the string on a tree in your yard for the birds.

Practicing Peacemaking

As a family, take a few moments to think about people in your lives who are not easy to get along with. In our own family, sometimes that was brother to brother. Talk about how the Pilgrims and Indians made peace. Think about how different they were from each other and how that would complicate things. Think of at least one nice thing you can do for someone who is hard to get along with.

Making Life-size Indians and Pilgrims

Using a large piece of paper, trace around your young child. (Newsprint is great to use. Tape two sheets together if necessary.) Let the child color and decorate as a pilgrim or an In-

143

dian. Cut out the Indian or Pilgrim and put it on the wall. Ask your child, "Who do you identify with the more—the Indians or the Pilgrims? Why?"

Thanksgiving—A Sharing Time

The Pilgrims were generous and shared their blessings with others. How can you as a family share with others this Thanksgiving? Consider the following:

Mayflower Baskets

Let the children decorate a basket. Fill the basket with goodies that an elderly friend could use:

- Canned food
- Fruit
- Nuts
- Stationery
- Stamps
- Assorted cards (birthday, get well)

Take the basket to an elderly friend or neighbor. Put the basket on the doorknob or by the door. Ring the door bell and hide!

The Pineapple Turkey

A special way to say "I'm thankful for you" to a teacher or special friend is to give a pineapple turkey. Mr. Turkey makes a quick and easy centerpiece—plus he's practical and may be eaten later.

Mr. Turkey's head is simple to make for anyone learning to sew.

Materials needed are

- One fresh pineapple with bushy leaves
- Felt (brown, red, white, and black)
- Thread
- Popsicle stick
- Scissors and glue

Adopt a Family for Christmas

Think about a family you know that has special needs at this time of year. If you don't know such a family, check with your church, the Salvation Army, or a local welfare agency. Invite your adopted family for Thanksgiving dinner. In December you can provide toys and other gifts to help make their Christmas special.

Help with a Feast for the Poor

As a family, volunteer to help with Thanksgiving dinner for the poor. Check with local welfare agencies, the local rescue mission, or the Salvation Army. While you would probably not do this every year, it is a great experience for your family to have at least once.

Thanksgiving—A Working Together Time

Thanksgiving is a great time to include your family in the preparations. Too many times when we are doing special things for our family—like cooking Thanksgiving dinner—we are impatient when they seem to "get in our way." I've been known to yell, "Now, get out of the kitchen and stay out of the kitchen—and I mean it!" One mother in a MOM's support Group shared her solution. She lets each child choose one dish to make for Thanksgiving dinner. She does as much preparation as possible ahead of time—usually the day before.

Even a simple contribution will help the child feel included. One year this mom's five-year-old son got excited about fixing beans! With Mom's help he opened the can of green beans and "cooked" them in the microwave. Because they were sharing Thanksgiving dinner with a family across town, they put the beans in a dish, stored them in the refrigerator overnight, and took them to the family Thanksgiving dinner the next day. (Yes, they had to reheat the beans the next day, but her son was so proud and actually ate them too!)

Her other son chose to make gumdrop bread. "It tasted awful," she said, but the children loved it! Should you want to try something so exotic, here's the recipe:

Making Thanksgiving Gumdrop Bread

Ingredients:

¾ cup tiny gumdrops
3 cups flour
¾ cup sugar
1 tablespoon baking
   powder

1 egg
¼ teaspoon salt
1⅓ cup milk
⅓ cup cooking oil
½ teaspoon vanilla

Directions:

1. Preheat the oven to 350 degrees. Generously grease a loaf pan. With kitchen scissors, cut the gumdrops in half. (If your scissors start sticking together, dip the blades into a glass of cold water.) Put the cut gumdrops into a large mixing bowl.

2. Put the flour, sugar, baking powder, and salt into the mixing bowl with the gumdrops. Stir with a wooden spoon until well mixed. Set the mixture aside until you're ready to use it.

3. Crack and beat one egg in a small bowl. Add milk, oil, and vanilla. Beat until well mixed.

4. Pour the egg mixture into the flour mixture. Stir until the dry ingredients are wet. The mixture should be lumpy, so do not stir too much. Put the mixture into greased loaf pan. With a rubber scraper, scrape the bowl and spread the mixture evenly in the pan.

5. Bake for 60 to 65 minutes. To see if the bread is done, push a wooden pick into the bread near the center. If the pick comes out dry, the bread is done.

6. Set the loaf on a cooling rack. Run a metal spatula around all 4 sides of the pan. Turn the pan on its side. Shake the pan gently to remove the bread. Set the pan aside, and turn the bread right side up. Cool the bread completely before cutting. Makes one loaf.[1]

To add a festive atmosphere to your Thanksgiving celebration, let your children make unique place cards.

 Thanksgiving Cornucopia Place Cards

A clever place card can be made with colored construction paper, one Bugle™ (a horn-shaped corn snack), glue, and small dried flowers or weeds. Baby's breath works well.

Cut the construction paper into pieces 3 by 4 inches. Fold each in half lengthwise. Glue one Bugle™ on each card. Fill the Bugle™ with dried flowers, and glue them in place. Write a name on each card with a felt-tip pen. Presto! You have unique place cards for the Thanksgiving dinner table.

Thanksgiving—A Time for Considering Your Heritage

One Thanksgiving we were guests in the home of a large family. As we all sat around the table, our hostess asked who could tell the story of the first Thanksgiving. Piece by piece, the story began to emerge—part fact and part fiction. Amidst the laughter we realized that it is up to us as parents to pass down the heritage and history of Thanksgiving.

 ### Reading About Thanksgiving

Read the Thanksgiving story to your children. Books suggested by MOM's Support Group mother's are

- *The First Thanksgiving Feast,* Joan Anderson (this is an easy reader) (New York: Clarion/Ticknor & Fields, 1984).
- *Thanksgiving Day,* Robert M. Bartlett (New York: Crowell Jr. Books/Harper Jr., 1965).
- *How Many Days to America,* Eve Bunting (New York: Clarion/Ticknor & Fields, 1990).
- *Arthur's Thanksgiving,* Marc Brown (Boston: Little, Brown, 1983).
- *Thanksgiving at the Tappletons,* Elie Spinelli (New York: Trophy/Harper Jr., 1989).

The following books are all available from Oleanna Books, Box 141020, Minneapolis, MN 55414.

- *It's Thanksgiving,* Jack Prelutsky

- *My First Thanksgiving Book,* Jane B. Moncure
- *Squanto and the First Thanksgiving,* Joyce K. Kessel

Thanksgiving—A Time for Looking Ahead

The two days immediately after Thanksgiving are often "down times" and can be perked up by beginning preparations for the next major holiday on the horizon—Christmas! It's a great time to plan your Christmas Advent Celebration—and make the Advent wreath.

Advent begins four Sundays before Christmas and goes through Christmas Eve. (Some calendar years, the first Sunday of Advent is the first Sunday after Thanksgiving, so this is a timely activity.) Let me encourage you to make Advent a time of getting hearts and homes ready for the celebration of the birth of Christ. To make Advent more meaningful for your family this year, make an Advent wreath.

Making an Advent Wreath

To make a wreath:

- Choose a circular base of Styrofoam™, wire, or wood, with holes for four candles. The circle represents eternity.
- Attach the evergreen branches to the base. The ever-

149

greens stand for everlasting life and hope. (Artificial greenery will do just fine.)
- Add pine cones, holly, or other decorations.
- Insert four candles. The four candles of the Advent wreath represent four Sundays of anticipating Christmas.
- Put a large candle in the center of the wreath. This candle represents Christ, the light of the world.
- Light one candle on the first Sunday, two candles on the second Sunday, etc.

As the candles' light grows brighter each week, so will your desire to celebrate the coming of Jesus—the light of the world.

Why not make the celebration of Advent the cornerstone of your Christmas traditions. It can become a welcome oasis from the secular rush and commercialization of Christmas.

In the hustle and bustle of getting ready for the holidays, take the time to focus on your family and say "thank you" for all the positive things you see. Thanksgiving can become one holiday to experience all year long!

10

Christmas

Do you ever feel someone rewrote the Christmas script like this: "And it came to pass in those days that there went out a decree from the trend setters, the advertising agencies, and the Joneses down the street that all of America should go shopping. And all went out to shop, each to his own mall (or discount store)."

Remember when Christmas used to be in December? It gets earlier each year. Green and red decorations hit the stores in early October, and Christmas trees are at the corner market before Thanksgiving. In our neighborhood, the lights and decorations go up in November when it's still 70 degrees outside!

Not only do we jump the gun in decorating for Christmas. Nowadays, children get a head start on greed. Whatever happened to the kids who sang, "All I want for Christmas is my two front teeth"?

It's easy to feel stress at this time of year. You still remember last year when the children fought over their presents, the dog ate the turkey, and Aunt Gertrude wouldn't speak to Uncle Albert.

Or you've been to six stores but still can't find that doll your five-year-old expects to see under the tree on Christmas morning. At this point, all *you* want for Christmas is a simple holiday stress reliever!

Instead of peace on earth and good will toward humanity, many people find themselves in a frenzied cycle of working, spending, and preparing that accelerates right up to Christmas Day. Then comes the letdown as fatigue, unpaid bills, and guilt feelings over missing the real meaning of Christmas begin to surface.

One reason for holiday stress is wanting Christmas to be perfect. We picture one big happy family gathered around the tree surrounded by just the right gifts. Snowflakes gracefully fall outside while inside the aromas of turkey, ham, and mincemeat pies fill the house—which, of course, is immaculate and looks like the December issue of *House Beautiful*.

What are your expectations for the coming Christmas season? Do you picture a storybook Christmas complete with elves and perfect harmony? Take a few minutes and check out your expectations.

Expectation Inventory

My expectations for this Christmas Season are

1.
2.
3.
4.

Now look at your list and answer the following questions:

- Are my expectations realistic?
- Which expectations can I control?
- Which expectations are beyond my control?

Remember, storybook Christmases are just that—and should be reserved for the pages of storybooks! How can we keep our expectations realistic? How can we control the holidays instead of their controlling us? May I suggest something really radical? Practice the four P's of peace at Christmas—pray, plan, prepare, and preserve!

Pray

A meaningful Christmas will begin on our knees. In James 1:5, we read that if we lack wisdom we are to ask God for it and He will give it to us liberally. Only the Lord can give us balance. We want to emphasize the real meaning of Christmas without becoming grinches and taking all the fun out of the holidays for our children.

In Christian families, we stress the spiritual side of life all twelve months. We don't just teach Scripture to our children in December. Sometimes in an attempt to balance the secular emphasis of this time of year, we outlaw anything red (that has a beard) and give our children an overdose of what we feel is appropriate. At the other extreme, the family totally forgets whose birthday it is anyway!

Balance is wonderful, but so rare in today's world! We know it is more blessed to give than to receive, but try to convince a four year old! Presents are just a part of Christmas, so how can we keep things in balance? Start by praying! As we bring all our problems and concerns to the Lord, He will give peace and balance to Christmas celebration. Then we will be ready to move on to the second P—planning.

Plan

As we commit ourselves and our Christmases to the Lord, we can count on Him to help us formulate our plans.

Choose Your Own Traditions

Neither Dave nor I came from families with lots of traditions. We were both of the generation that went to Grandma's, so we didn't do that much in our own homes to celebrate the holidays. As our children were growing up, we lived in Austria. Going to Grandma's wasn't an option, so we began to develop our own holiday traditions. We adopted some from Austria, some from friends, some from books—we almost overdosed on traditions. I am an overachiever mom, and I wanted to do it all!

Many people are so committed to tradition that they are determined to have creamed celery on Christmas Day—even if everyone hates creamed celery—because Aunt Annie always had creamed celery. Besides, traditions are important . . . aren't they? Yes and No. Yes, if we keep things in balance (there is that word again). No, if the traditions are conflict ridden and self-defeating.

Tradition Inventory

To find your balance, take a tradition inventory. List traditions you observe, and note the origin of each tradition.

Traditions We Presently Observe   Origin of Tradition

1.
2.
3.
4.

Which of the above traditions are not that meaningful?

1.
2.
3.

Traditions We Would Like to Start

1.
2.
3.

To expand this activity, you may want to group your traditions in different categories and then evaluate each, such as, baking, decorating, gift giving, spiritual emphasis.

Family Tradition Inventory

Vary the tradition inventory exercise by doing it with your children. Let them tell you their favorite traditions and their least favorites.

Setting our own traditions became a tradition in the Arp Family. You will want to do the tradition inventory exercise from time to time. As our family grew and the boys entered college, married, and moved into their adult lives, our traditions began to change. This was not always easy for me. I experienced anew what Solomon wrote in Ecclesiastes: There is a time for everything. We might paraphrase and say that there is a time for building traditions, and there is a time for letting go. This past Christmas was our first without all three sons here to celebrate. Life changes, but memories live on.

Observing a tradition doesn't mean you have to do the same thing the same way every year. The memory is a funny thing. You may only do things a certain way one year, yet years later in your child's mind that was a tradition! Someone said a tradition is anything you do twice!

Let me encourage you to take the time now—this year—to choose which traditions you are going to celebrate and what you are going to drop.

Planning for Family Time

Along with assessing traditions, assess how you are spending your time. We can get so busy doing things for our families that we neglect spending time with them. Did you know that the four weeks that separate Thanksgiving and Christmas are the four weeks family members are most ignored? Why? We're so busy shopping, decorating, and cooking for our families that we spend less time with our families. Here is another holiday stress reducer.

What I'm Going to Do

List the things you know for sure you want to do this holiday season:

1.
2.
3.
4.

Now think about the things you are not going to do. Last year you went to the *Nutcracker Suite;* this year you really want to visit the living Christmas tree or the nativity pageant. You can't do everything every year! Just as important as planning what we are going to do is planning what we are not going to do. Often the problem is trying to do too many "right" things.

What I'm Not Going to Do!

List the things you do not want to do:

1.
2.

3.

4.

Now take your list of things you want to do and prioritize it. Put a big star by the things that are not negotiable. This is your number one list. Now place a two by the next most important thing and a three by the third most important.

As in the tradition inventory, you may want to repeat this exercise for different kinds of Christmas activities. For cooking, for example, list those things that would result in the cancellation of Christmas if you didn't have them. At our house that would be molasses cookies and chocolate fudge. Now list the things it would be awfully nice to have around.

Look at your cooking plan, and consider how to bring family members into the cooking scene. When our boys were young, I gave each of them a coupon for making Christmas goodies with Mom. They got to choose their favorite Christmas goody and spend time cooking alone with Mom. Just think, they could sift all of the flour, put on all of the sprinkles, and lick all of the bowl! To this day gooey caramel candies remind me of Joel and our cooking times together. This is one Christmas activity that may have rich dividends in later years. One Christmas Joel and Jeanne gave us a wonderful Christmas present—they took control of our kitchen and completely prepared Christmas dinner. (As a gift to them, we cleaned the kitchen after the meal!)

 ## Just-Me-and-Mom Cookie Bake

Let your child choose a favorite recipe. Bake the cookies or make the candy alone with one child!

Here's a simple cookie recipe:

Paintbrush Cookies

Mix thoroughly:

⅓ cup soft shortening
⅓ cup sugar
1 egg
⅔ cup honey
1 teaspoon vanilla

Stir in

2¾ cups sifted flour
1 teaspoon soda
1 teaspoon salt

Directions: Chill the cookie dough. Heat the oven to 375 degrees. Roll the dough out to ¼-inch thickness. Cut it in different shapes. Bake 8 to 10 minutes on a greased baking sheet. For clear colors, do not let cookies brown. Makes 5 dozen 2½-inch cookies.

Paint designs with egg yolk paint.

Blend well 1 egg yolk and ¼ teaspoon water. Divide the mixture among several small custard cups. Add a different food coloring to each cup to make bright colors. Paint designs on the cookies with small paintbrushes. If the egg yolk paint thickens on standing, add a few drops of water.

If you do not have the time to make cookies from scratch, you can purchase rolls of sugar cookie dough. Roll out this dough and proceed with directions above.

Plan for Free Time!

I used to feel that if I had an hour free, I had an hour to fill up with some other activity. Not so! What happens to many of us today is illustrated in the following diagram:

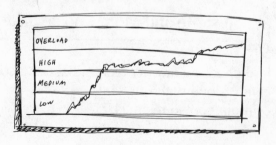

What I did was plan my time in the high zone. It worked fine as long as no one got sick, changed plans, had a special problem, or sneezed. The moment anything was added to my "to do" list, I went straight into overload. In my memory there is no tiredness so tired as that feeling on Christmas afternoon after I did it *all!*

Let me encourage you to keep your plans in the medium range and even plan in a few low-range days. The unexpected is just that—unexpected. But it happens.

Your own December calendar will help you get a good overview of what you can realistically do. It will also create anticipation as you plan with your family for this wonderful time of year. I am including a sample calendar from the Arp family archives. Note the many easy suggested activities. Be creative and have fun with your own unique December family calendar (see pp. 160–161)!

Warning: Contrary to what the ads say, December is not the ideal time to remodel your kitchen, add a new room—to have more room for the holidays, of course!—or finally put down your dream carpet. However strong the urge, try to resist starting new projects in December.

Plan to Simplify Gift Giving

Another area we need to simplify is gift giving. How can we plan now so that in January and February we will not be staring at huge, depressing bills? One family we know limits gifts to twenty dollars. They also went back to the old tradition of giving each person one gift!

For several years we have been working on simplifying the gift-giving part of Christmas. One wise friend whose children are now grown gives this tidbit of advice: Save big presents for the child's own birthday. My friend did not say this out of any economic pressure. Her husband is a surgeon, and as she put it,

159

December

SUN	MON	TUE	WED	THU	FRI	SAT

Behold, what manner of love the Father has bestowed on us,
that we should be called children of God!—1 John 3:1

December

SUN	MON	TUE	WED	THU	FRI	SAT
		27 Family Planning. Discuss what we'll do, what we won't do.	**28** Set up Christmas Factory (with wrapping supplies).	**29** Pull out Christmas decorations!	**30** Hang Advent Calendar.	**1** Draw names for Advent Secret Pals. Do 1 kind deed a day until Christmas.
2 Light 1 Advent candle Read Isaiah 9:2, 6 John 8:12	**3** Set up Nativity Scene.	**4** Family Night Make your own Christmas cards.	**5** Give a compliment!	**6** Read the story of St. Nicholas.	**7** Draw names for stockings. Set $10 limit. (For families with older kids)	**8** Create 'n Bake Day!
9 Light 2 candles Read Luke 2:4-7	**10** Open Christmas cards together. Pray for each family.	**11** Make someone smile.	**12** Read aloud as a family.	**13** Get in shape! Exercise as a family.	**14** Make a snowman. (If no snow use styrofoam & cotton balls).	**15** Invite someone who lives alone to dinner.
16 Count your blessings!	**17**	**18** Take holiday lights tour of your community.	**19** Call someone you rarely see.	**20** Light tree & candles. Play Christmas music & be silent 10 minutes.	**21** Make gifts-of-love coupons (babysit, yardwork, shop, etc.).	**22** Celebrate 1st day of winter with cookies & hot chocolate.
23 Light 4 candles Read Luke 2:15-20 John 1:1-12	**24** Light 4 candles; then light the Christ candle. Read Luke 2:1-20	**25** Take turns opening gifts. Celebrate His Birthday!	After-Christmas Tips: • Put together a Christmas puzzle. • Take a "group nap" around the Christmas tree. • Watch a football game (if you must). • Enjoy your family—now!			

"Everyone's situation has pros and cons. When our children were growing up we didn't have to deal with economic worries, but we had to be creative since Dad was often away at the hospital and rarely home." The Arps' situation was the opposite. We got our exercise squeezing pennies, but we did have more time to spend with our boys than did those in many other professions.

Homemade gifts.   Consider making some of your gifts. You don't have to be a great cook, seamstress, or crafts person to make a personal, thoughtful and meaningful gift. Many times it is simply a matter of putting several items together and tying them up with a cute ribbon. Here are some suggestions of home-made gifts you can make with your children:

A Gift of Spiced Tea

Combine

    1 large jar of Tang™
    1 large package Country Time Lemonade™
    1 large jar sweetened and lemoned tea
    Ground cloves to taste
    3 tablespoons cinnamon.

    Mix and fill containers. Decorate with a bow or tree ornament.

A Gift of Seasoned Salt

1 box iodized salt   1 ounce garlic powder
1½ ounces black pepper   1 ounce chili powder
2 ounces red pepper   1 ounce Accent™

Combine and place in a bottle or jar with a tight-fitting lid. Makes 32 ounces. Divide into small jars for gifts. Baby food jars are a great size.

A Gift of Festive Apple Bread

Ingredients:

1 egg	1½ cups plain flour
1 cup sugar	1 teaspoon cinnamon
1 stick butter	2 cups fresh apples
Dash of salt	(diced)
1 teaspoon baking soda	

Mix all the ingredients. The batter will be thick. Bake it in loaf pans for 45 minutes at 325 degrees. You can also bake it in miniature loaf pans. Give the bread and the pan as a gift.

Spool Candlesticks

Buy spools at an antique market. Add candles and bows. They cost about three dollars each.

Cinnamon Baskets

Use an orange juice can, a rubber band, ribbon, and cinnamon sticks. Cover the can with cinnamon sticks, using the rubber band to hold the cinnamon sticks in place. Tie with festive ribbons. Fill with pecans, cashews, or peppermint candy.

Peppermint Play Dough

Ingredients:

3 cups flour
1½ cup salt
6 teaspoons cream of
  tartar

3 cups water
3 tablespoons Wesson™
  oil
Peppermint extract

Sift the dry ingredients into an aluminum pan. Add the liquid. Blend well. Cook over moderate heat until the dough pulls away from the pan. Be sure to stir constantly! When the dough cools enough to handle, knead it on board with the peppermint extract. Divide and knead in various colors (you can use food coloring) to get the desired shades. Store each color in an airtight container. The play dough will last up to 3 months if refrigerated. Tie up in a ribbon with a cookie cutter for a special gift for a special child!

Fragrant Pomander Balls

Supplies needed:

- 1 orange
- 1 small box of whole cloves
- colored ribbons

Tie ribbons around the unpeeled orange so that the fruit is quartered, with ribbon ends streaming down. Pin the ribbon in place. Press cloves, stem-first, tightly together into the orange until fruit is covered. Tie handling ribbon from the top. The cloves will preserve the orange. As it shrinks, it gives off a festive aroma. Tighten the ribbons after one week.

Making a Photo Album for Grandparents

If you have cleverly saved negatives of your favorite candid family snapshots, have copies made for a special album for grandparents.

If you are like our family and have no idea where the negatives are, you can take your colored pictures to a quick print shop and have colored copies made. You may be amazed at how nicely they turn out. This process is also great when you need the pictures immediately! Usually there is no waiting, and you can go home with your colored copies!

Giving Coupons of Service

Each coupon may be cashed in for certain activities or things you know the recipient would appreciate. The best gifts don't have to cost lots of money. Sometimes we give the best gifts when we give of ourselves. Possible coupon service gifts are

- Baby sitting coupons
- House cleaning service
- Baking a favorite dessert
- Teaching a child how to build a birdhouse
- Setting the table each evening for a week

One creative mom added this suggestion: Give older family members and friends who don't need more "things" a

Goody-of-the-Month certificate. Each month she bakes a different "goody" and delivers it with a personal visit.

Inexpensive gifts.   What about gifts for nieces, nephews, cousins, and other friends? Realistically, you can't make them all, so I've included suggestions from other mothers of what's current today:

Games—always great gifts

Consider these:

- Hot Potato—This is a simple one, but you get to throw this stuffed potato around, so it's a crowd pleaser.
- Pictionary Junior Play It with Clay—This guess-the-word game is just like its cousin except that you use clay to make the clues.
- Domino Rally—You set the plastic dominoes up and watch them tumble down in patterns.
- Slap Happy—Each child gets a huge, brightly colored foam hand, and you see who can slap the right color dot first.

Puzzles—Berenstein Bears, Duck Tales, and lots of puppies and kittens for little children. One set that looks wonderful is My First Giant Jigsaw Puzzle. The puzzle of Big Bird has nine pieces and is 21 inches tall and 14 inches wide when completed!

Other inexpensive gift suggestions:

- Koosh balls—Even kids who already have some of them seem to want more! They come in all sizes.
- Play-doh Fingles—These little kits give you the fun of Play-doh without the whole factory. You mold finger puppets in the molds and can then play with them. For ages 4 and up.

- Rug hooking kits—Children ages 8 to 12 can make small rugs in a variety of designs with these kits. Most of the designs look girlish, but a boy might be convinced to make one for Mom or Grandma.
- Pottycraft—Air-dry clay makes this a good gift for the artistic child in the family. You get three pounds of air-dry clay, enough to make a pot or vase, and it doesn't have to be fired. Paint and glaze is also included.
- Don't forget Legos and other such building systems. There are even holiday kits for building an angel, a reindeer, or a snowman.[1]

As our family grew older, we added a tradition that involved our boys more in giftgiving than giftgetting. For years Dave and I had faithfully stuffed stockings for each of our sons. They were delighted and we enjoyed doing it, but the older they got, the more unbalanced it seemed because we had no stockings to be stuffed! The following activity, suggested by a mom in a MOM's Support Group helped to bring balance and added fun to a new tradition at our house.

Stocking Stuffer Name Draw

For families with older children, put everyone's name in a hat—parents included—and draw names. Each person is responsible for stuffing the stocking of another family member. Set a price limit like ten dollars per stocking.

Our stocking stuffer tradition was so much fun that it has continued through the years. As adults, we still stuff each other's stockings. Well, to be perfectly honest with you, it has been fun most years—except for the year one brother gave another brother a generous can of cat food. The memories could have been worse if we had not stopped the disappointed cat food owner from smearing cat food all over a certain brother's bedroom!

Prepare

Preparation for Christmas officially starts in November with the making of the Advent wreath (see pages 149–150). To help children visualize how many days it is to Christmas, you might make a Christmas countdown chain.

Christmas Countdown Chain

Cut different colors of construction paper into strips 1 by 6 inches. Write a number on each from 1 to 25. Then make a chain by gluing the strips together in the correct order. Hang the chain in a prominent place (like in the kitchen) and let children take turns tearing off one loop each day.

The Christmas season moves into full swing when we begin to accumulate gifts. Many times the challenge is to hide the gifts before others discover them. The sooner they are wrapped, the less the snooping—or at least that was the way it was when our boys were young. And half of the fun is wrapping and decorating the gifts. It was just the mess I disliked! To combat all the clutter, lost tape, scissors, and other wrapping items, we created a Christmas factory.

Creating a Christmas Factory

Choose a special room or corner in your home where you can keep supplies for wrapping gifts and creating Christmas specials. Possible supplies include: paper, ribbon, scotch tape, scissors, Styrofoam™, glitter, glue, buttons, stickers, boxes, and so on.

For money stretching packaging suggestions, consider these:

- Plain brown bags with burlap ribbon, twine, or red and green yarn. Add Christmas symbols or holiday greetings with magic markers or stencils.
- Newspaper for large packages. Children love getting the comic sections.
- Decorate packages with pine cones, evergreen sprigs, or tiny tree ornaments.
- Make gift tags out of recycled Christmas cards.

Making Chrismons for the Tree

Chrismons are Christian symbols that have been passed down through the years. Following are various patterns for making ornaments for your Christmas tree. You can cut the Chrismons out of Styrofoam™. Spray or outline them with glue. Decorate with gold or silver glitter.

CHRISMONS (Christian Monograms)

The Latin cross symbolizes the type of cross on which Christ was crucified.

The fish was a sign used by early Christians. The letters ΙΧΘΥΣ form an acrostic on the Greek phrase Jesus Christ, Son of God, Savior.

"But these are written that you may believe that Jesus is the Christ, the Son of God, and that believing you may have life in His name" (John 20:31).

The first and last letters of the Greek alphabet stand for Jesus Christ.

"'I am the Alpha and the Omega, the Beginning and the End,' says the Lord, 'who is and who was and who is to come, the Almighty'" (Rev. 1:8).

The circle and triangle represent the eternity of the Trinity.

"For there are three who bear witness in heaven: the Father, the Word, and the Holy Spirit; and these three are one" (1 John 5:7).

"Before the mountains were brought forth,
Or ever You had formed the earth and the world,
Even from everlasting to everlasting, You are God" (Psalm 90:2).

The scroll symbolizes the Pentateuch, the Law, the first five books of the Bible.

"'Do not think that I came to destroy the Law or the Prophets. I did not come to destroy but to fulfill'" (Matt. 5:17).

The lamp symbolizes the Word of God.

"Your word is a lamp to my feet
And a light to my path" (Psalm 119:105).

"There shall be no night there: They need no lamp nor light of the sun, for the Lord God gives them light. And they shall reign forever and ever" (Rev. 22:5).

The descending dove with a three-rayed nimbus (halo) around its head is a symbol of the Holy Spirit.

"When He had been baptized, Jesus came up immediately from the water; and behold, the heavens were opened to Him, and He saw the Spirit of God descending like a dove and alighting upon Him. And suddenly a voice came from heaven, saying, 'This is My beloved Son, in whom I am well pleased'" (Matt. 3:16–17).

The cross and crown symbolize that Jesus Christ is King of kings and Lord of lords.

He humbled Himself and became obedient to the point of death, even the death of the cross. Therefore God also has highly exalted Him and given Him the name which is above every name, that at the name of Jesus every knee should bow, of those in heaven, and of those on earth, and of those under the earth, and that every tongue should confess that Jesus Christ is Lord, to the glory of God the Father" (Phil. 2:8–11).

Making Dough Ornaments

Mix together

2 cups flour
1 cup salt
1 cup water

Knead together. Roll out and cut with cookie cutters. Brush with beaten egg. Punch a hole in each ornament before baking. Bake at 300 degrees.

Push red and green yarn or ribbon through the hole and make a tie for each ornament. Leave the ornaments natural or paint them with acrylic paints. Spray varnish for a lovely finish.

Making Ice Cream Cone Trees

Supplies Needed:

- Cone-shaped ice cream cone
- Can of frosting
- Blunt knife
- Assortment of small candies and sprinkles (red hots work great!)

Stand the cone over for a tree shape, ice with frosting, and decorate with candies and sprinkles.

Making a Yearly Family Scrapbook

Designate December as scrapbook month. Save all your favorite snapshots through the year. Pull them out in December and make a scrapbook of your year. It's also the time to pull out scrapbooks from previous years and enjoy the memories of years gone by. In one family we know, making the scrapbook is Dad's special job.

Making a Snowman without Snow

Sad that you don't have a white Christmas? That won't stop you from making a snowman! Use cookie dough, cotton balls, or Styrofoam™. Definitely use your imagination!

Taking a Holiday Tour of Lights

Take a tour of your community. Let the kids plan the route. If you are really energetic, make it a walking tour.

Straw in the Manger

Assemble your nativity scene at the beginning of December. We had two nativity scenes, one china, to "look at," and one which the children could hold and touch. This activity is for the nativity scene that you can touch.

Leave the manger empty and have a small container of straw near by. As each child does something she feels is loving and kind, she adds a straw to the manger. On Christmas Day, when baby Jesus is laid in the manger, your children will appreciate that their kind deeds help to prepare His bed.

Brown Bag Party

Have an impromptu brown bag Christmas party. Roll down the tops of brown lunch bags, and fill each bag with goodies to munch around the tree. You could use nuts, dried fruit, popcorn, miniature muffins, and cookies. Put on your favorite Christmas tape, light the tree, and take a few minutes to enjoy each other and the magic of this time of year.

Birthday Cake for Jesus

Bake a birthday cake for Jesus, and share it on Christmas Eve or Christmas day. Explain the symbolism to your children:

- White, round cake represents the purity of Jesus.
- Twenty red candles in a circle on the cake.
  Twenty candles represent the twentieth century since Christ's birth.
  Red candles represent the blood Jesus shed for us on the cross; red is also a color of Christmas joy.
  The circle represents the unending (eternal) reign of Jesus Christ.
- Lighted candles remind us that Jesus is the light of the world.
- A silver star in the center of the cake represents the star of Bethlehem that the shepherds and wise men saw (can be made with silver candles or by covering cardboard with aluminum foil).
- An angel in center of cake reminds us of the first angel that told the good news of Jesus' birth.

Sing "Happy Birthday" to Jesus and blow out the candles.

Scripture Names of the Lord

Take turns looking up the Scripture passages and reading

Matthew 1:16	Christ
Hebrews 6:20	High Priest
Acts 2:32–36	Risen Lord
Exodus 3:14	I Am
Acts 20:28	Shepherd
John 3:2	Teacher
John 1:41	Messiah
Revelation 3:14	Amen
John 20:31	Son of God
Isaiah 9:6	Wonderful Counselor, Mighty God, Everlasting Father, Prince of Peace

---

Ten Minutes of Silence

Each evening before bedtime, gather around the tree. Light the tree and perhaps candles as well. Turn out the electric lights, play Christmas music, and observe ten minutes of silence. We found this was a wonderful way to "soothe the wild beast," and bedtime was much calmer and more pleasant.

176

Persevere

What do you do when you can't seem to "soothe the wild beast" in your home? With changes in schedules and routines, kids can become hyper and bored. It's easy to eat too many sweets and to feel we have too much to do. At times like these, we need to remember the last P at Christmas time: to persevere. Can you identify with the mom who wrote the verses that follow?

The Christmas Lament

Two days before Christmas and all through the house,
There is so much to do, I feel like a louse.

The stockings are hung all over the chair;
The clothes are all dirty; there's nothing to wear.

The kids are not sleeping, but fighting instead;
It looks like me and pa will never get to bed.

The cookies need baking; there's shopping to do.
If Christmas is so great, why am I so blue?

Maybe it's time for you to take a mini break and try some stress relievers. Give your body a chance to relax. Consider the following:

Holiday Stress Busters

- Take a warm bath. Warm water calms you by increasing circulation and relaxing muscles.
- Breathe deeply. When anxiety strikes, the heart races; breathing deeply will help you relax.
- Take a walk around the block.
- Build a fire, turn on soft music, and have a cup of hot chocolate or hot tea.

177

- Have a quiet time. Read your favorite passage of Scripture or read Psalm 23.
- Keep your sense of humor.
- Write in a journal. Sometimes summing up the day's or week's highs and lows will help you laugh at them and keep things in perspective.

 **Celebrating Christmas Afternoon**

Take time to wind down as a family. Each year we have a Christmas puzzle that we begin to put together on Christmas afternoon after all the celebrating is over.

Also consider pulling out the sleeping bags and taking a family nap around the Christmas tree. It's time to relax!

As you anticipate this coming Christmas, let me encourage you to pick and choose from the suggested activities. You can't do them all. Please don't try! Be your own architect. Be realistic. Expect some joy, expect some tears, expect some frustrations, but also expect God to meet you and your family in a special way as you seek to honor Him this holiday season.

11

Easter

Society hasn't paganized Easter; Christians have Christianized a pagan holiday. Did you know that the Easter celebration, named after a pagan goddess of spring called Oestre, began before the birth of Christ? It was the celebration of the annual reawakening of the earth's fertility after the long, cold "death" of winter. So Christians have taken a pagan custom and used it to teach spiritual truths.

After the Resurrection, families faced a real dilemma. How could they point their children to the wonderful truth of God in Jesus Christ? Could they actually use the pagan elements to teach spiritual truths? In the old pagan festival they observed the underlying theme of thankfulness for the new life that comes to the earth each spring. They decided to use it as a natural object lesson that pointed to the resurrection of Jesus from the bonds of death. Even the *World Book Encyclopedia* says they were successful. *World Book* describes Easter as "A Christian festival that celebrates the resurrection of Jesus Christ. Easter is the most important holy day of the Christian religion."[1]

So for us in the twentieth century, Easter continues to be an opportunity to let the traditions and symbols of that old festival take on newer, fuller, and deeper meanings as they point to our risen Lord. Just remember, when people talk about celebrating the real meaning of Easter—we are celebrating much more!

Seven Days to Easter

Starting on Palm Sunday, follow Jesus' footsteps. Choose an unhurried time when the family can be together each day, possibly in the evening before bedtime or right after dinner. Read the appropriate Scripture passages for each day. Discuss what you read and talk about the objects listed for each day.

Day 1—Palm Sunday
   Subject: Jesus entering Jerusalem
   Scripture: John 12:12–19
            Mark 11:1–11
   Object: Palm branch or other greenery
        Donkey
        For young children: Let's have a parade. Pretend Jesus is coming to town. Make banners; blow up balloons. Pull out the rhythm band and have a parade!

Day 2—Monday
   Subject: Jesus at the temple, turning over money changers'
       tables
   Scripture: Mark 11:15–19
           Matthew 21:12–17
   Object: Coins

Day 3—Tuesday
   Subject: The withered fig tree, prayer, faith, forgiveness
   Scripture: Mark 11:12–14; 11:20–25
           Matthew 21:18–22
   Object: Fig tree, figs (Use your imagination; use another
       kind of tree and fruit if you want. You could substi-
       tute dates for figs.)

Day 4—Wednesday
    Subject: Woman anointing Jesus; Judas agreeing to betray
           Jesus
    Scripture: Mark 14:1–11
           Matthew 26:6–13; 26:14–16
    Object: Perfume (if using felt, pour some perfume on the
           felt.)
           Thirty silver coins (You can use nickels, dimes,
           quarters, or play money.)

Day 5—Thursday
    Subject: The Lord's Supper, foot washing, Garden of Geth-
           semane
    Scripture: Mark 14:17–26, 32–42
           John 13:1–17
    Object: Bowl, soap, towel, grapes or grape juice, bread

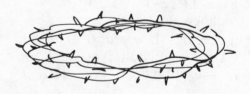

Day 6—Friday
    Subject: The Crucifixion; the burial
    Scripture: Luke 23
           Matthew 17:1–61
    Object: Cross, crown of thorns (made from a rose bush)
           Dice, sponge, nails

Day 7—Saturday
Subject: The tomb; prophecy of Crucifixion
Scripture: Matthew 27:62–66
            Isaiah 53
Object: Stone, lamb, tomb

Day 8—Sunday
Subject: The Resurrection, the empty tomb
Scripture: Matthew 28:1–5
            Luke 24:1–49
Object: Angel, bread

Depending on the ages of your children, use objects in one of the following ways:

- Make a felt board. Each day cut out suggested objects in felt and place them on the felt board.
- Each day hide objects for that specific day, and let your children hunt and find them.
- Use things you can find around your home. For instance a toy donkey, real coins, artificial greenery. Display ob-

183

jects on the table as you have your discussion. Each day put the objects in a large Easter basket.[2]

- Talk about different symbols, and let children draw and color them.
- Encourage your children to come up with other symbols that remind them of Easter.

To make your time together special, light a candle. Talk about how Jesus is the light of the world.

Easter Egg Traditions

The custom of exchanging eggs began before the birth of Christ. The Egyptians and Persians dyed eggs in spring colors and gave them to their friends to celebrate new life.

The early Christians were the first to use colored eggs at Easter. Later, in Europe, Christians colored eggs red to represent the shed blood of Christ and the joy of the Resurrection.

The tradition of writing messages and dates on eggs began in England. Fancy candy eggs with windows and tiny scenes inside were popular gifts in the 1800s.

For us today, dying and decorating eggs can become an opportunity to teach our children of new life offered by God in Christ. Consider some of the following activities.

 Dyeing Eggs Together as a Family

Hard cook the eggs before dyeing them. Let the children write messages or draw pictures or use Easter stencils on the eggs. Use tape if you want to have two-tone eggs. Be creative and have fun.

Decorating an Easter Egg Tree

For the tree, use a branch just as it is or spray paint it white. You can also use sprigs of pussy willow or forsythia blossoms. Put them in a vase or container, and you have an Easter egg tree all ready for decorating.

Make your own egg decorations. Use real eggs. Punch a small hole in both ends of a raw egg. Use an ice pick to break the yolk. Holding the egg over a bowl, blow on one end. With a little effort the yolk and white of the egg should be forced out of the other end of the egg and into the bowl. (This is a good evening to have omelettes for dinner.)

Paint the eggs any color that you like. Place the eggs in an old egg carton and let them dry. You can use acrylic or oil paint. Decorate any way you want. You can paint designs on the eggs—hearts, flowers or curlicues. You can use rickrack, borders, stencils, yarn, felt, or whatever you like. One year one of our boys cut out little pieces of felt and made an empty tomb on his egg.

Cut yarn into eight-inch lengths. Thread the yarn through a large needle and push it through the two holes in each egg. Tie a large knot in the end at the bottom so the yarn will stay and not pull through. Use the other end of the yarn to tie the egg onto the tree.[3]

Another fun Easter activity is to fill plastic eggs with symbols of Easter. Let the children take turns opening the eggs and telling about the symbol inside. You share last, and save one egg that is completely empty. Talk about the empty tomb.

Five Special Eggs

Use plastic fill-and-thrill eggs

- Yellow (stands for light)—On the outside, stick a sticker of either a candle or the sun. On the inside place a little scroll with this Scripture, "I am the light of the world" (John 8:12). Also include a little surprise such as an eraser shaped like a candle or light bulb.
- Purple (stands for royalty)—Put a crown sticker on the outside. On the inside, a Scripture scroll with 1 Timothy 6:15: "The King of kings and Lord of lords." A surprise could be a crown pin or ring.
- Pink (stands for love)—Outside stick a heart and cross sticker; inside, a Scripture scroll with John 3:16, "For God so loved the world that He gave His only begotten Son," and a surprise of a cross pin or ring.
- Green (stands for new life)—Put a butterfly sticker on the outside. Inside put a Scripture scroll with Romans 6:4: "Christ was raised from the dead by the glory of the Father, even so we also should walk in newness of life." Add a surprise, anything with a butterfly on it (for instance, a pin or ink stamp).
- Blue (stands for peace)—Outside, stick a dove sticker. Inside, put a Scripture scroll with Isaiah 9:6, "Prince of Peace," and a dove pin.

Most of these stickers and little gifts can be found at a Christian bookstore.

Easter Story in an Eggshell

Supplies Needed:

- Large white plastic egg (that you can buy pantyhose in)
- Easter basket grass
- Popsicle stick broken into 2 pieces and glued together to make a cross
- Baby doll to represent Christ. (You can make one out of a tiny ball of fiberfill covered in nylon hose and wrapped in blue fabric. Draw on a face with a pen, and use yarn for the hair.)
- Tiny artificial flowers
- Ribbon, lace flowers to decorate outside of egg

Easter Cookies

Make rolled cookies and cut out as crosses, flowers, candles, eggs, lambs, and empty tomb. Decorate.

See recipe on page 158 or use rolls of dough.

Hot Cross Buns on Good Friday

Hot Cross Buns[4]

Ingredients:

2 packages active dry yeast	³/₄ teaspoon salt
½ cup warm water	3½ to 4 cups sifted flour
¼ cup scalded milk	½ to 1 teaspoon cinnamon
½ cup salad oil or melted shortening	3 beaten eggs
⅓ cup sugar	⅔ cup currants
	1 egg white

Preheat your oven to 375 degrees.

Soften the dry yeast in warm water. Combine milk, salad oil, sugar, and salt; cool to lukewarm. Sift 1 cup of the flour with the cinnamon; stir into the milk mixture.

Add the eggs. Beat well. Stir in softened yeast and currants. Add the remaining flour or enough to make a soft dough, beating well. Cover the dough with a damp cloth and let it rise in warm place till double (about 1½ hours). Punch it down. Then turn it out on a lightly floured surface. Cover it and let it rest 10 minutes. Roll or pat it to ½ inch. Cut it in rounds with floured 2½-inch biscuit cutter. Shape it into buns. Place them on a greased baking sheet about 1½ inches apart. Cover and let rise in a warm place till almost double (about 1 hour).

Cut a shallow cross in each bun with sharp scissors or a knife. Brush the tops with slightly beaten egg white. Bake the buns in a moderate over (375°) 15 minutes or till done. Cool slightly, and frost. Makes about 24.

188

Icing for Hot Cross Buns

Add about ¾ cup powdered sugar to remaining egg white. Pipe it on the crosses. For a tube, roll a sheet of paper to form a cone; snip off the end. Fill it with frosting; squeeze.

As you enjoy eating the Hot Cross Buns together, talk about how the cross reminds us of Christ's death on the cross and the yeast is a symbol of new life.

Enjoying Easter Music

Each year teach your children one new Easter song, such as "Christ the Lord Is Risen Today." Talk about the meaning of the song. For young children, who can't read the hymnal, it will be fun for them to learn the words that are being sung.

At home, preschoolers enjoy singing and acting out the Easter song "He Arose." As you sing quietly and slowly, "Low in the grave He lay," squat down. Then jump up as you loudly sing, "Up from the grave He arose!"

Mom might ask, "What about Peter Cottontail?" With all the fun activities centered around the spiritual truths of the Easter message, our family never gave a lot of attention to Peter Cottontail. It wasn't that we disliked him; he just wasn't that important or significant. We treated him the way we did the tooth fairy. We had fun and just let him hop down his bunny trail.

In the meantime, the Arps seized the opportunities of the Easter season to teach and appreciate the wonderful unique Christian message of new life in Christ and new beginnings. We hope you will do the same.

Part Five

Making It Work

12

Putting It All Together

I'll never forget the first winter of our long-awaited empty nest. The adolescent avalanches, elementary storms, and preschool panics were memories. Once again we were eating brussel sprouts, lima beans, and asparagus (all the vegetables that our youngest son, Jonathan disliked).

Friends often asked us, "How are you adjusting to the empty nest?" We responded, "It's not that bad!" We didn't realize how well we had adjusted to being "two" again until all our adult children plus wives came home for a winter visit.

We were delighted at the thought of an Arp family reunion. Everyone is spread out around the country, and it's not often that we can all be together at the same time. But we were not so delighted when we found out they all wanted to bring their cats—a total of five!

Did we actually agree to host this "cat convention"? Yes, but under duress. In discussing the possibility of getting all the family cats together, Joel said over the phone, "Mom, think about it—it's a chance to build one more memory!" How could we say no to that?

We went right out and bought a cat condo so that all the cats would have a fun place to play and sleep—and perhaps ignore our furniture. You see, we are not, and have never been, a major "indoor pet" family. We did have our share of hamsters, guinea pigs, and goldfish, but living in an apartment in Austria didn't encourage major pet ownership.

By the time we moved back to the states, our children were older, and we realized any cats or dogs we might adopt at this stage of life would outlive our kids' childhood years. Also we pet sat enough to know who would actually have to care for a pet, and neither Dave nor I was interested. So we never gave in to our boys' attempted blackmail—they threatened that they would be emotionally damaged for life because they never had cats or dogs. We kept saying, "When you grow up, you can have all the pets you want." The rest is history. They'd taken our suggestion—and they were all coming to visit us!

Sitting at our kitchen table, looking at our new cat condo, we asked each other, "Are we crazy?" Could we survive the onslaught of five adults and five cats? Were we headed for a severe winter storm?

The situation we found ourselves in is not unlike your present dilemma. You've made it through most of the pages of *Beating the Winter Blues*, and maybe you're already following a plan. But halfway through your winter you've been derailed by something unexpected (like the arrival of our five cats). What do you do now? It's no longer a matter of beating the winter blues—we're talking survival! Let me warn you as you begin your planning process and launch into your winter: All your plans will not fly. Some days you will feel like giving up.

Be Flexible! Be Prepared!

Plan for flexibility. You may want to collect a list of things that are simple to do and require very little of your time. Recently I asked the mothers in a MOM's Support Group, who have just lived through another winter, to tell me their favorite Minute

Mother Helper tip. (A Minute Mother Helper is an activity that takes little time for you to set up and will keep your child occupied for at least twenty minutes.) Here are some of their creative suggestions:

Making a "You-Can-Eat-It" Necklace

Give each child a bowl of Cheerios and a bowl of Fruit Loops (or any cereal with a hole in the middle) and a string. Let your children create their own special necklaces. Then, with a glass of juice or milk, let them eat their necklaces! (Don't let them eat the string.)

Paint-by-Water Books

Keep a couple of paint-by-water books in reserve for special times you need a break. Give your child a cup of water, book, and paintbrush. If you don't have a paintbrush handy, moms say that Q-Tips work great and are a lot less messy than brushes.

Fun with Beans

One mom shared: "I always found cooking dinner a chore, because my two-year-old became a leech on my leg, crying, asking me to hold him, asking for juice—you get the picture.

So I filled a large Tupperware mixing bowl with dried beans of all the kinds I could find: brown beans, white beans, and lentils. I added a wooden spoon for stirring and plastic cups for scooping and pouring inside the bowl.

"When I need some time, I give him the bowl. I guess for a little boy it's like sitting outside playing in gravel. He loves playing with the different beans and mixing them up. When he's done, I put the lid on it and put it on top of the refrigerator until later. This is a great activity for my child because he can sit at the kitchen table and be close to me."

 ## Colored Chalk Creativity

A big box of colored chalk and a child's great imagination make for lots of fun with sidewalk or driveway art! They love it, and the rain (or hose) will eventually wash it off.

 ## My Own Kitchen Drawer

Moms of toddlers love this one! Keep a special drawer that is low and easy for your toddler to open and close. Store plastic containers and tops—anything that doesn't break—and let your toddler play until her heart is content! This is great when Mom is busy preparing dinner. (A pots and pans drawer is also fun. The young child loves the noise, which is fine if Mom doesn't already have a headache.)

Treasure Hunt

Hide objects throughout your home. Give your child a paper bag, and let him or her have fun hunting for treasures. Objects suggested by moms:

- Pennies—Let the children keep the pennies they find.
- M&M's—Let the children eat M&M's they find.
- Healthy snacks like carrot or celery sticks (This didn't work at our house, but one mom I know has two children ages nine and twelve and has resisted giving her children sugary snacks all those years, so I guess it's possible!)
- Hide pieces of a big, super-simple puzzle. The child can find the pieces and then put the puzzle together.

Dress-Up Clothes Box

A box of dress-up clothes (hats, dresses, purses, scarves, belts, and shoes) can keep kids busy for a long time. An old slip makes a great wedding dress! Make sure there is a full-length mirror close by so they can admire themselves and their "finery."

Let's Type

"Not every mother would let her children do this," says one MOM's Support Group mother, "but I have an older typewriter, and I let my child type. Since he's just learned his alphabet, he loves this. All I have to do is put the paper in the typewriter!"

Cookie or Pizza Bake

When older children or teenagers have a friend over, let them bake cookies or pizza. The kitchen will be a mess, but it will give them something inexpensive to do—and you won't have to drive them anywhere!

Pretend Tea Party

Give your small child paper cups, napkins, plates, and cupcake papers for a pretend party. She can invite all her favorite stuffed animals.

Even these simple ideas take some time and planning. But when you tend to get tired and disappointed, remember why you are doing this.

What's Your Motive?

You are not just surviving the winter or filling up the winter days with activities. Instead you are in the process of facilitating lives, of building relationships with your children that will span a lifetime, of building memories that you will all treasure in the future. What you are doing is vital to your family's health and well-being.

Beating the Winter Blues and its counterpart, *Sanity in the Summertime*, give you the resources to plan, prepare for, and actually enjoy the active parenting years. Don't just take my word for it. Listen to what mothers who have been involved in planning their winters and summers for years are saying today. One mom shares: "Planning for the winter has helped me focus on what is really important. As a young mom, I planned weekly menus and my daily agenda of errands, but I never considered planning goals for my children. It's easy to get busy and slide from one activity to the next and unknowingly miss opportunities for quality time with our children.

"When our three sons were one, three, and five, my main goal was to get the diapers changed and the garbage out! It was about that time that I began to get together with a few other mothers who were in the same boat. We used the book *Sanity in the Summertime* and began our own little MOM's Support Group. We challenged each other to think about things that were really important. I received feedback and encouragement, and my confidence as a mom began to grow as I had access to hundreds of ideas like the ones included in this book.

"Now my boys are nine, eleven, and thirteen. I can honestly say that this approach to parenting—setting goals, actively planning, and being encouraged and supported by other moms—has made a tremendous difference. My advice to you is to take the time to plan, to set goals, and to build the relationship with each of your children. Consider joining or forming your own MOM's Support Group. Believe me, it's one of the best investments of time you will ever make!"

A mother of a seven-year-old son and a ten-year-old daughter adds: "I got involved in setting goals and planning for my family through MOM's Support Group years ago when my daughter was a baby. At that time it seemed family life would go on and on and I would forever be changing diapers and cleaning up messes. But now I realize how fast the years go by. As I look toward the future—yes, now I believe one day we will have an empty nest—I observe different reactions from moms who are already there. Some seem to view life as empty; others face the future with an attitude of "Boy, it's been fun! I'm ready to move on to the next stage of life." I hope I will face the empty nest—just about eleven years up the road for me—with the latter reaction.

"Using the ideas in this book and in *Sanity in the Summertime,* and my involvement in MOM's Support Group over the years, helped me make the most of and enjoy to the fullest every day and every stage. Without sounding trite, I can say I relish every bit of it. I already have a rich feeling of a wealth of memories—not just vague recollections.

"Why do I feel this way? It's certainly not because I've done it all right, I don't qualify for super mom, and at times I get migraine headaches that I have to live with. I feel the way I do because I have invested time with my children instead of just spending time with them. There is a big difference. Let me encourage you to use the resources that are available to you to invest in building positive relationships with your children. Don't feel you have to do it all! All the suggestions in this book will not be for you, but choose the ones that fit your own unique situation to enrich your family relationships. You won't be disappointed. I'm finding that I'm receiving dividends all along the way, and someday I'll look back and say, 'Boy, it's been fun! Hard work—but fun!'"

Face it—parenting is hard work, but it can be fun. Let me encourage you to take the advice from these two moms. And as you build your winter memories, be prepared for some joy and some frustration as well. For example, back to the visit of the five cats.

The Cat Saga Continues . . .

All our adult sons arrived with wives and cats. We definitely built memories, and we found that the bad comes with the good! Some of our memories from that visit are great ones—the hours

200

and hours of the whole family sitting on the stairs and the floor of the upstairs hall playing with the cats! Oh, yes, the cat condo was a big success.

Some of our memories are funny ones—like the time Jarrett and Laurie's cat, Posner, climbed the wallpaper to get upstairs rather than taking the traditional steps! Some memories are not so pleasant—like the time cat Zooey ate the pumpkin pie, or when cat Faustus left his unique signature on a bedspread (to this day a slightly beige reminder of his visit remains), or the unintelligible autograph on the wooden piano bench by Mr. Anonymous Cat.

We'll never forget when Jeanne and Joel's two cats, Pete Dogmatic (so named because he's all black and white) and Sebastian decided to play hide and seek in our attic right before their owners were getting ready to leave.

Was it fun? At times, we have to say yes. Are we glad we did it? We think so. It was the one visit we remember when our frustrations centered around cats and not family members and personalities! No one complained of being bored or having nothing to talk about. There were no arguments or overheated discussions. There was always a cat or two around to laugh at!

So would we do it again? We're not sure! We'd never commit ourselves to something like that in a book, but to be honest, we probably would.

Making Choices

As you think about this winter, you'll also have choices to make. Whatever your plans, count on some joy, and count on some tears and disappointments. But it will all add up to unique memories for you and your family. Enjoy the fun times. Tolerate the hard times. Weather the storms. And remember, spring is coming!

Looking at wintertime from the vantage point of the empty nest, I ask myself, "If I could put life into reverse—go back and do it all over again—what would I do differently?"

First, I'm not sure I would have the energy! Second, I would probably just make different mistakes the second time around. This I do know: I'd try to enjoy the process a lot more. I asked myself this question recently, and here's one mom's list of "If I had it to do over again":

If I had it to do over again, I'd bake more cookies and sit down more often with my children to eat those cookies.

I'd try to answer more questions and admit it when I didn't have the answers.

I'd laugh more with my kids and laugh more at myself.

I'd have a messier house, complain less, and close more doors.

I'd worry less about mud and snow tracks on my carpet. I'd put on my boots and mittens, join the kids for a snow ball fight, and make angels in the snow.

I'd let my kids help more with the holiday baking. We might even make gumdrop bread.

I'd compare less, judge less, worry less about the outcome of my kids—and worry less what others think.

After all, did all my worry and uptightness help? What message did my fear and lack of trust communicate? Yes, if I had it to do over again, I'd trust more, give more honest compliments, look more for the positive, and overlook some of the negative. After all, no one is perfect! I just wouldn't take myself quite so seriously. I'd be a moment-by-moment mom, for quickly—so quickly—the moments pass away.

As you look at the coming winter, let me encourage you to use your remaining moments as a resident mother to love, enjoy, build up, and encourage those unique characters in your home. Don't miss out on the joys of motherhood while you're living through it. Now is the time to build for the future. Now is the time to beat the winter blues!

Notes

Chapter 1   Beating the Winter Blues

1. From Ann Landers, *The Knoxville Journal*, 21 Feb. 1986, A-8.

Chapter 2   Planning for Wintertime Sanity

1. Jean Grasso Fitzpatrick, "How to Slow Down," *Parents Magazine*, Apr. 1989, 98.
2. Ibid.
3. Ibid., 99.
4. Adapted from Dave Arp and Claudia Arp, *60 One-Minute Memory Builders* (Nashville: Wolgemuth & Hyatt, 1989), 60.
5. Adapted from Linda Dillow and Claudia Arp, *Sanity in the Summertime* (Nashville: Thomas Nelson, 1990), 60.

Chapter 3   To Know Me Is to Love Me

1. Lawrence M. Kutner, "Don't Fret about Mistakes, Parents Urged," *Knoxville News-Sentinel*, 3 Nov. 1990, B-1.
2. Bonnidell Clouse, Ph.D., "Your Child Today", *Christian Parenting Today*, 55.
3. Adapted from *Virtue Magazine*, Jan./Feb. 1991, 58.
4. Dillow and Arp, 33–34.
5. Clouse, 55.
6. Claudia Arp, *Almost 13* (Nashville: Thomas Nelson, 1986), 39–40.
7. Adapted from Arp and Arp, *60 One-Minute Memory Builders*, 15–16.
8. Ibid., 17–18.
9. Ibid., 25–26.
10. Charles Swindoll, *You and Your Child* (Nashville: Thomas Nelson, 1977), 42.

Chapter 4   Developing the Big *R*

1. Jerry White and Mary White, *When Your Kids Aren't Kids Anymore* (Colorado Springs, CO: NavPress, 1989), 19. Used by permission.
2. Sharon K. Johnson, "All Around the House," *Christian Parenting Today*, May/June 1989, 23.
3. Jean Lush with Pamela Vredevett, *Mothers and Sons* (Old Tappan, NJ; Fleming H. Revell, 1988). Used by permission.
4. Johnson, 25.

5. Kathy Collard Miller, "The Big *R*," *Christian Parenting Today,* May/June 1990, 40.

6. Ibid., 41.

7. Adapted from *Family Life Today,* Jan. 1981, 35–36.

Chapter 5   Breaking Away and Letting Go

1. Some activities adapted from Laurie Winslow Sargent, "Things as Jimmy Sees Them", *Christian Parenting Today,* Mar./Apr. 1990, 12.

2. Arp and Arp, *60 One-Minute Memory Builders,* 25.

3. Adapted from Arp, *Almost 13,* 141–50.

Chapter 6   Schooltime Sanity Savers

1. "The Parent's Guide to Back-to-School Cool," *Woman's Day,* 4 Sept. 1990, 120.

2. Gary Sinclair, "What Can Parents Do When a Child Won't Study," *Family Life Today,* Oct. 1982, 49.

Chapter 7   Sports: Whose Game Is It?

1. J. R. Bishop and Cliff Schimmels, *Sports and Your Child* (Nashville: Nelson, 1985), 69.

2. Ibid., 25–26.

3. Points 1–4 adapted from ibid., 18–19.

Chapter 8   Snow Days, Sick Days, and "We've-Got-Nothing-to-Do" Days

1. Adapted from Sherri Gardner Howell, "There's No Party Like a Snow Party," *Knoxville News-Sentinel,* 29 Dec. 1990, B-3.

Chapter 9   Thanksgiving

1. Adapted from Better Homes and Garden, *Step-by-Step Kids' Cookbook* (Des Moines, IA: Meredith, 1984), 64–65.

Chapter 10   Christmas

1. Adapted from Sherri Gardner Howell, "Rhymes & Reasons," *Knoxville News-Sentinel,* 24 Nov. 1990, B-3.

Chapter 11   Easter

1. *World Book Encyclopedia,* ed., s.v. Easter.

2. Adapted from *Family Life Today,* Apr. 1984, 27–29, and *Virtue Magazine,* Mar./Apr. 1990, 35–36.

3. Arp and Arp, *60 One-Minute Memory Builders,* 145–146.

4. "Hot Cross Buns," *Better Homes and Gardens New Cookbook* (Des Moines, IA: Meredith, 1962), 62.

Index of Activities
and Exercises

205

Just-Me-and-Mom Times

*(These activities are appropriate
for one-to-one times but many are
great for the whole family.)*

Super Easy Activities

(These activities are great when you are exhausted and are willing to invest ten minutes or less to have your child busy for twenty minutes or more!)

About the Author

Co-author of *Sanity in the Summertime*, Claudia Arp is founder of the MOM's Support Groups, a family enrichment resource program with groups throughout the United States and in Europe. Claudia has also authored *Almost 13*. She and her husband, Dave, are cofounders and directors of Marriage Alive International, a marriage enrichment ministry, and co-authors of *Ten Dates for Mates*.

The Arps are parents of three sons and two daughters-in-law and live in Knoxville.

Resources Available
from Marriage Alive

Building Positive Relationships with Children

MOM's Support Group is a proven, family enrichment resource that is providing moms with supportive friendships and helping them build positive relationships with their children. MOM's is being used by churches and small groups across the United States and in Europe to help moms enjoy motherhood while they live through it!

Endorsed by:
· Josh McDowell
· David & Vera Mace
· Stephen Brown
· Dr. D. James Kennedy
· Vonette Bright
· Jeanne Hendricks
· Dr. Howard Hendricks

Package includes:
Leader's Guide
Study Books
Videos

Building Positive Relationships for the Adolescent Years

This versatile program includes a five-part video series, a Leader's Guide and Parent's individual study book.

Endorsed by:
· Jeb Bush · Rosey Grier
· Don Schula
· Edward James Olmos
· Informed Families of Dade County, Florida
· Family Foundation of Savannah

Mom's & Dad's Support Group is being used by schools, churches and groups across the country, to help parents relate to other parents and offers practical guidance in preparing for and surviving the adolescent years.

For More Information write:
Marriage Alive International, Inc.
P.O. Box 90303, Knoxville, TN 37990
or call (615) 691-MOMS or 691-8505